Y0-BST-480

TEACH YOURSELF BOOKS

HERALDRY AND GENEALOGY

TEACH YOURSELF BOOKS
HERALDRY AND GENEALOGY

L. G. PINE
B.A.(Lond.), F.S.A.Scot., F.J.I., F.R.S.A., F.R.G.S.

Fellow of Royal Asiatic Society
Barrister-at-Law, Inner Temple
Formerly Editor: *Burke's Peerage, Burke's Landed Gentry,
Landed Gentry of Ireland, International Year Book*, etc., etc.

Illustrated by W. J. HILL

TEACH YOURSELF BOOKS
ST. PAUL'S HOUSE WARWICK LANE LONDON E.C.4

To
RICHARD LESLIE PINE

First printed 1957
This edition 1970

ISBN 0 340 05614 2

Made and Printed in Great Britain for The English Universities Press, Ltd., London by C. Tinling & Co. Ltd., Liverpool, London and Prescot

CONTENTS

	PAGE
PREFACE	ix

CHAPTER ONE   11
   What is Heraldry? Various definitions. The Origin of Heraldry in Western Europe and its possible traces in other parts of the world.

CHAPTER TWO   24
   The language of Heraldry. The Anglo-French words and terms which are used. The reason for the use of French in this connection. The division into metals, colours and furs.

CHAPTER THREE   30
   The make-up of the coat of arms or armorial achievement. The shield, crest, mantling, supporters, helmet, motto and the charges on the shield.

CHAPTER FOUR   40
   The language of symbolism in western heraldry and instances of a play on words (canting heraldry) and cases in which the origin of the charges can be traced.

CHAPTER FIVE   48
   The development of Heraldry in western Europe. Were arms invented for themselves by the original users or were they granted? The earliest written evidence. Rolls of Arms.

CHAPTER SIX   55
   The earliest heraldic literature in Britain and in Europe. Early English treatises on Heraldry

CHAPTER SEVEN   62
   The end of Mediaeval Heraldry with the Wars of the Roses. The growing control of coats of arms by Kings who set up Colleges of Arms.

CHAPTER EIGHT   67
   The Heralds' Visitations. The control of arms from the 15th century onwards. The Court of Chivalry.

CHAPTER NINE   79
   The Court of Chivalry, its abolition, and its restoration after the restoration of the monarchy in 1660, discontinuance in 1735 and revival in 1954–55.

PAGE

CHAPTER TEN   87
    Tudor Heraldry and the use of coats of arms without armour in decoration in a more extensive manner than during the Middle Ages.

CHAPTER ELEVEN   98
    The stagnation of Heraldry in the later 17th and 18th centuries. The position in Scotland and Ireland.

CHAPTER TWELVE   105
    A short account of Welsh, Scottish and Irish Heraldry.

CHAPTER THIRTEEN   116
    The Heraldic Revival in the 19th century.

CHAPTER FOURTEEN   120
    Heraldry in the United States.

CHAPTER FIFTEEN   127
    The present position of Heraldry:
        (i) In Britain and the Commonwealth.

CHAPTER SIXTEEN   137
    The present position of Heraldry:
        (ii) In other parts of the world

CHAPTER SEVENTEEN   143
    The rudiments of Genealogy. Genealogy inseparable from Heraldry.

CHAPTER EIGHTEEN   150
    The study of Genealogy in England.

CHAPTER NINETEEN   158
    Questions and Exercises.

GLOSSARY   163

INDEX   188

ILLUSTRATIONS

		PAGE
1.	Luttrell Psalter	15
2.	Bayeux Tapestry	16
3.	Enamel of Count Geoffrey of Anjou	17
4.	Seal of John Warenne, Earl of Surrey, 1301; obverse and reverse	18
5.	Chinese Monad and Japanese Mons	20
6.	Shields showing furs, ermine, vair ancient, vair modern and potent	26
7.	City of Jerusalem, showing exceptional metal on metal	27
8.	Shakespeare, arms granted to John, father of William	28
9.	D'Arcy arms showing chapeau; shield couché and bouche	32
10.	Chetwynd-Stapylton arms showing privileged use of supporters	37
11.	Arms of Stourton	41
12.	Gurges for Gorges	42
13.	Lord Crook of Carshalton, arms granted 1947	43
14.	Lucy arms: canting coat with old type of pear-shaped shield	46
15.	Carminow, Grosvenor, Scrope, (4 coats)	52
16.	Arms of College of Arms	69
17.	Nine cadency marks	77
18.	Cardinal Wolsey, Archbishop of York, arms of	80
19.	Bodiam, Wardedieux and Dalyngrigge from Bodiam Castle	87
20.	Stained glass window, Clare arms, Salisbury Cathedral	88
21.	Stained glass window, Salisbury, showing arms of Warwick the King Maker	89
22.	Brass of Sir John Dabernon, Stoke Dabernon, Surrey	90
23.	Shield from tomb of Edmund of Langley, 5th son of Edward III, King's Langley, Herts.	92
24.	Shield of Sir Winston Churchill, K.G., showing augmentations granted to his ancestors	93
25.	Encaustic tile from floor of Tewkesbury Abbey: Beauchamp of Bergavenny	94
26.	Viscount Nelson, K.B., arms of; a 19th century heraldic monstrosity	103
27.	New Badge of Wales, augmented 1953	107
28.	Arms of Aldershot	129
29.	Westminster Bank, arms of	131
30.	Atomic Energy Authority, arms	133

ACKNOWLEDGEMENT

The Author and Publishers acknowledge the courtesy of Messrs. Gale & Polden Ltd. in granting permission to quote from Col. Howard N. Cole's book, *The Story of Aldershot*.

PREFACE

THIS book was originally written in 1956, published in 1957 and has been given two small revisions since. Now, however, the publishers have asked me to revise the work throughout. In making this necessary revision, I have been struck by the enormously increased interest in heraldry which has manifested itself over the last 14 or 15 years. The Congress movement to which I referred in 1956 as a new feature in heraldic study has now become a regular event in the minds of all who are interested in the subject, so that people tend to make arrangements to see each other at the next Congress in two years' time. As for the United States, interest in heraldry grows apace, and the American College of Arms is now a reality.

Many excellent studies have been made of specialized heraldic matters, and these again reflect the growing interest in the subject. The substitution of republics for monarchies instead of signalling the death of heraldry, has given fresh impetus to its devotees, and encouraged them to band together, in order to maintain the knowledge of the science in their own land.

It remains for me to say, as in all my other works, that I shall be greatly obliged to those who will be kind enough to send to me any notes or queries with regard to the text of the volume; from my many correspondents all over the world, I have learned a very great deal, and I am thus indebted to them. If delay occurs in answering a letter, I beg them to understand that the pressure of correspondence does not always enable me to reply quickly.

L. G. PINE.

Bodiam, High Street,
Petworth, Sussex.

CHAPTER ONE

WHAT IS HERALDRY?

*Various definitions. The Origin of Heraldry in
Western Europe and its possible traces in other
parts of the world*

M OST people are attracted by rich colour and nowhere is
rich colour more likely to be found in modern life than in
heraldic emblems. Millions must have seen the statues of the
Queen's Beasts outside the Abbey at Westminster during
Coronation time, many thousands must have seen the Heralds
of the College of Arms at various functions, such as a State
Opening of Parliament, a Proclamation, etc.; while there are
enormous numbers of people all over Great Britain and Western Europe, not to mention other parts of the world who
frequently in their daily life see examples of heraldic symbols,
coats of arms, crests, and other items, which fascinate and, at
the same time, intrigue them. For confronted with: *Argent a
chevron sable between three water bougies gules, a chief azure
thereon three cross crosslets of the first*, most people retire
justifiably baffled, with the feeling that here is something very
interesting but unfortunately closed to them owing to the
difficulties of the subject which only the experts can understand. It is a pity, because a few days of study can give the
ordinary intelligent man or woman sufficient insight into the
meaning of Heraldry to make every walk in every British town
or village a matter of enhanced interest. Heraldry is not, most
emphatically not, a subject of abstruse research like atomic
physics. The subject of coats of arms has been curtained over
with a rich shroud of mystery on the part of some writers,
partly from a desire to keep the public from penetrating too
deeply into the matter, and partly through the dullness and
lack of skill of the writers themselves. To-day these conditions
no longer apply. Several expositors of heraldry have made it
very illuminating by using essentially modern methods to
describe it. Sir Iain Moncreiffe, for instance, has not hesitated
to employ the strip cartoon technique to the illustration of

Heraldry, which shows that it is not necessary to abandon this particular art form to the mercies of the popular Press.

First then, what is Heraldry? The shorthand of history, some reply, which does not help very much because the definition itself requires explanation. "Science of a herald" is the definition given in the Concise Oxford Dictionary; to which a reader will naturally object that it does not tell the whole story. But the Concise Oxford goes on comfortingly to add: "Armorial bearings". There in a nutshell we have our first difficulty. When we speak of Heraldry we usually mean coats of arms, crests, etc., and not merely the ceremonial or other functions of a herald. But originally, and strictly speaking now, the word "Heraldry" meant as the Dictionary says, the science or duties of a herald; only later did the word come to mean also the terms and descriptions of the art which the herald had to administer. There were coats of arms in plenty long before there were any recognised heralds, and the word used to describe arms, their meaning and use was "armory". You can still find this in the dictionary but it is hardly ever used to-day except in the title of an old reference book, *Burke's General Armory*, and by a few antiquarians. It would be pedantic to revive the word armory now, so we can continue with the term we know, Heraldry, to denote, not only the functions of the herald, but also the use and description of the things, the coats of arms, which he administers, or studies.

It is important to get these definitions clear at the start, and so although we shall deal at proper length in chapter 3 with the constituents of the coat of arms, I would like to remove one misconception now. People very often say that they have a crest, when they mean that they have a coat of arms, and I have known some of my clients in Burke to declare that they possess a crest but are not sure that they have a coat of arms. This is all nonsense. A coat of arms is the correct term for the whole armorial achievement. This includes, shield, helmet, crest, mantling, and sometimes supporters. The essential part is the shield without which there cannot be a coat of arms, the crest is merely an addition made much later, as we shall see in chapter 3. As to the term coat of arms, that is derived from the practice in the Middle Ages for the armour of the knights to be covered over with a coat of linen or in some cases of silk. This covering was used to protect the armour from rust and dirt and also to protect the wearer from the effects of the sun's rays pouring on to the steel. On these covers the arms of the wearer were embroidered and hence the term coat of arms.

You will observe that we have referred to coat armour and the Middle Ages. Heraldry is essentially mediaeval in its origin and is associated with all the images which we conjure up when we think of the Middle Ages. Knights in armour, castles, lovely ladies and princesses, tournaments, dragons, enchanters, giants, all the apparatus of old romance, yes it is with these things that Heraldry is linked. It is one of the survivals of the mediaeval period. At Canterbury Cathedral can be seen the shield of the Black Prince, not so far away at Bodiam Castle, the perfect castle of the Middle Ages, there are the arms of Bodiam, Wardedieux, and Dalyngrigge families over the great gateway. (See page 88 for more detail). All very picturesque and having no relation to the modern age? Well, every time that you watch a television programme put out by the B.B.C., the arms of the Corporation appear on the screen at the beginning of the afternoon or evening performance. Nothing could be more typical of modernity than the flying machine, and yet in the Royal Air Force there are hundreds of Badges which are the distinctive mark of the different units, such as squadrons and other formations. Badges and not crests are used by Air Force units and are designed to bear some allusion to the services or associations of those units, many of them in the words of Sir Gerald Wollaston, formerly Garter King of Arms, being "happy adaptations of symbols and heraldic charges which are both decorative and allusive." As an example of the adaptability of Heraldry, it may be observed that while Crowns of various types have been long used in different branches of Heraldry, the Kings of Arms (of the College of Arms) devised during the last war a new Crown indicative of association with the air. This Crown is called an Astral Crown and consists of wings and stars alternating. It was sanctioned by King George VI for No. 1 Flying Training School, and it is also available to be granted to distinguished officers of the Air Force and to persons or corporations especially connected with aviation, whether military or civil.

Thus Heraldry, which goes back to the remoter regions of

European history has been adapted down the ages to deal with bodies which would have been inconceivable outside the range of wizardry in the Middle Ages.

When did the use of coats of arms begin? It is a fairly safe answer to say, in Western Europe in the 12th century. But in dealing with a question of this type we have always to remember that the modern habit of dating and recording, especially through the daily newspaper, does not go back very far. If some new phenomenon were to appear in our time, it would inevitably get a place in the newspapers, on the front page, or in a lowlier place but it would be mentioned somewhere because it would be news. The phenomenon of flying saucers is an example. Consequently if anyone in 100 years time wants to write a history of the flying saucer movement, if we may use such an expression, he will find all he wants in the files of the newspapers at Colindale, the British Museum repository for back numbers of periodicals. In the 12th century, however, no daily journals were published and the few historians were usually the monks who did not go out of their way to chronicle things unless they were either of enormous national importance or were concerned with the affairs of the monastery. No one bothered to write about the origin of coats of arms, any more than anyone bothered to describe the changes in body armour from 1066 to 1485. We gather our information on these subjects from incidental records, the brasses in churches, the carvings on the tombs, the illustrations in stained glass windows, the illuminations in documents, or books, the seals of the kings and great men, and apart from these incidental sources, we have also the rolls of arms of the early heralds which date from about 1240 (see chapter 5). An example of the type of evidence is given in the MS. of the Luttrell Psalter, which in an illuminated miniature shows the figures of Sir Geoffrey Luttrell with his wife and daughter-in-law. Sir Geoffrey's arms are shown in several places in the drawing, these arms being described as *azure a bend between six martlets argent*. Both the ladies show the Luttrell arms on their gowns impaling (this means that the shield or coat of arms is divided down the middle with one coat on the right side and the second coat on the left side) the arms of their own father's families. Another case of the contemporary evidence which is available for those who study arms is in the great east window of Gloucester Cathedral which is described as the earliest war memorial in England. It was put up by one of the

Luttrell Psalter, *c.* 1340.

warriors of Crecy and contains at the base the arms of some of the fighters who were there in 1346. From such sources we are able to see what were the arms actually in use in the mediaeval period. It may be added that in the same way students of armour have to study the same sources for their subject.

Consequently when we say that the use of coats of arms arose in Europe in the 12th century we have to depend upon indirect evidence, which fortunately is forthcoming. The Bayeux Tapestry is a great help in this respect. It was made by the ladies of William the Conqueror and it shows the process of the Norman Conquest from the period of the latter part of Edward the Confessor's life until the end of the battle of Hastings. In this tapestry we have valuable contemporary evidence as to the styles of clothes and arms used in the period 1060-66. Now on the shields of some of the warriors as shown in the battle scenes there are designs, but these designs are not heraldic, a bird, a lion-like creature and a cross, all pictures which will appear later in true heraldry but which have also been seen on the shields of warriors since warfare has been chronicled. In many cases the shields bear what appear to be designs but which are seen on a closer look to be bosses made to support the shield and to strengthen it.

We have only to compare these designs in the Bayeux Tapestry with those seen in the Luttrell Psalter to see how greatly the latter differ from the rude Norman and Saxon drawings. This is not surprising in the course of 300 years. Fortunately we can bridge the gap with earlier illustrations before 1340. There is an interesting enamel which has the

The Bayeux Tapestry: Battle of Hastings.

portrait of Geoffrey Plantagenet, Count of Anjou, the son-in-law of Henry I. This shows the arms used on his shield and this shield was given to him by Henry I on the occasion of his marriage in 1127. Some golden lions appear on the shield, and as Geoffrey was the ancestor in the male line of the Plantagenets who were the first kings of England to use coats of arms these golden lions may in a sense be the forerunners of the lions on the royal arms used to this day. This enamel dates from about 1150 and it is the earliest example of an heraldic shield which we possess. Next to the enamel we have the evidence of the seals which in the period from 1135 to 1155 show the use of heraldic designs. Seals were used not only in the Middle Ages but much earlier to authenticate documents for those who could not read. In ages when few were literate there had to be some sign that men could readily understand to show that the person who was supposed to have produced the document had really done so. The seal which hung down from the document had to have on it something which gave the identity of the user of the seal. We have evidence of the use of

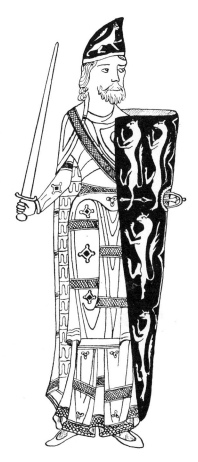

Geoffrey, Count of Anjou, father of Henry II,
with shield given him by father-in-law, Henry
I, in 1127.

seals as far back as the empires of the Babylonians and Assyrians and the idea was readily taken over into use in Europe before writing became fairly common. Thus though we often speak of King John having signed Magna Carta we ought really to say that he sealed it, for it is his seal and not his signature which is shown upon the document. Apart from the enamel which I have quoted above from 1150 the seals of arms constitute our earliest evidence of the appearance of coats of arms.

Seal of John, Earl of Surrey.
Baron's letter to the Pope, 1301.

What do I mean when I say that such and such a design is heraldic and another not, and that symbols have been used on shields in all ages, yet without being heraldic? Simply this, that for a design to be heraldic it must be hereditary. The designs used by a warrior of the Bayeux Tapestry such as Count Eustace of Boulogne are not the same as those of his descendants from which we infer that the Bayeux design was not intended to be hereditary. The whole essence of Heraldry is that the symbols used become hereditary and are passed down in families from father to son. This it is which differentiates them from the symbols used on the shields of warriors in past ages and in lands removed from Western Europe. The Greek warriors as depicted on the vases in the British Museum are shown with illustrations and drawings on their shields, and any boy who has suffered from construing the descriptions of Aeneas' shield in Virgil or Achilles' in Homer will know that those shields were decorated. Yet we know that among the Greeks and Romans the use of heraldic ensigns did not prevail. The Romans had a curious method of showing their ancestry. They used to have wax and later more permanent images in the halls of their homes, these images being representations of their ancestors who had held public office. A new man was one who had no ancestral office bearers. Among the Greeks there was a similar lack of the use of hereditary symbols, though it is fair to add that the present Garter King of Arms, Sir Anthony Wagner, thinks that some primitive form of heraldry prevailed among the great families of the 5th century B.C. in ancient Athens.

In all ages and countries of which we have any record there have been symbols used in war and in peace, but these are not the same as those which we call heraldic simply because they did not become permanent or hereditary. It is only in Western Europe that we find heraldic illustrations at the same time, in England, Scotland, France, Spain, Germany, Italy and the Low Countries, appearing about the same period (1135-1155) and continuing to spread. The common development does not mean that they are necessarily the product of a single mind. In all probability they originated from a utilitarian motive. For some time after the Norman Conquest armour continued to be mostly of chain mail and fairly light. The death of leaders, such as Harold at Hastings, from an arrow piercing his eye when unprotected by any face armour, or later (1199) the death of Richard I from an arrow piercing his shoulder, led attention to be given to the problem of more body protection for the knights. Certain it is as we can see from the illustrations in any good book on armour that very soon the helmet, instead of being open, closed over the face and gave additional protection, while the body was cased more and more in plate as against mail. Thus the knight received more protection but at the same time became less recognisable to his friends. Consequently it is probable that the use of coat armour developed from the necessity of knowing one's leaders in battle and tourney. It is a fact that the 12th century which saw the knight clad cap-a-pie in armour saw also the development of coats of arms on his surcoat, his shield, his lance pennon and banner.

Heraldry was not only confined to Western Europe but to

those sections of the half continent which were feudal and closely linked to the Catholic Church. Poland has Heraldry because primarily she is linked with the west through the fact that alone of the Slav nations she is Catholic, and has thus received western civilisation. In Ireland, Wales, and the Highlands of Scotland, Heraldry has been imitative, and the arms of ancient Celtic families will be found to be much more recent than the pedigrees of these families would seem to warrant. The reason is that the arms have been adopted in the later Middle

Chinese Monad.

Japanese Mon: family
of Tokugawa.

Japanese Mon: Emperor's
State Mon.

Japanese Mon: family
of Satsuma.

Ages in imitation of those of non-Celtic families which belonged to the western feudal tradition.

There is one important exception to the rule laid down above. In Japan for many ages the *mon* has been used which corresponds to the crest (part of the coat of arms in Europe) and is the family symbol of the Japanese people. In the Japanese peerage for the year 1912 in the British Museum library the account of every family is headed by its *mon*. Readers of fiction may recall Robert Standish's book, *The Three Bamboos*, in which the bamboo is the *mon* or crest of the

Fureno family. In Japan in the long feudal period during which the Mikado was kept a prisoner under the rule of the Shoguns all the conditions flourished which in Europe made the mediaeval period so picturesque and so uncomfortable for peaceful persons. The Japanese knights were certainly not less venturesome than their European counterparts and their ladies not less beautiful, added to which the Japanese had a love of fighting verging on the insane. The cult of Bushido was a grimmer chivalry. Heraldry could well flourish in such an atmosphere.

NOTES ON THE ORIGIN OF HERALDRY

There is a very large volume of literature on the subject of Heraldry but curiously enough the mystery which surrounds the birth of the subject seems to have been continued by most writers in modern times.

Heraldic books divide themselves into three classes. First, there are the very old treatises on Heraldry. These will be best dealt with later in our study, but some names may be mentioned here. Johannes de Bado Aureo (John of Guildford) wrote in about 1394 a *Treatise of Arms*; Nicholas Upton wrote about 1450 a Treatise, *de Studio Militari*. Then a few decades later there appeared the *Boke of St. Albans*, said to have been written by Dame Juliana Berners. A European writer of great importance was Bartolo de Sassoferrato, whose *Tractatus de Insigniis et Armis* was only one of his many works, for he was a great jurist and has a place in the history of international law. These authors are not the easiest to come by but we shall have more to say about them later on. They are certainly not a beginner's reading.

The foregoing books were written while coats of arms were used in the manner for which they had been designed. The second class of heraldic writer came much later. The knights in armour had practically passed away in the Tudor period, for body armour was worn in less enveloping forms and the many portraits which are preserved of armoured dignities are often merely a sitter's fancy. Among the books turned out in the 16th century in England on Heraldry there are Gerard Legh's *Accedence of Armorie* (1591), Guillim's *Heraldry*, and John Ferne's *Blazon of Gentry* (1573). (Accidence is here used in the sense of Grammar). These writers are accessible in large libraries, but again they are not good reading for beginners nor are they ever really good reading because the authors refused to understand that Heraldry was a practical thing and they embroidered the subject with ideas which had no basis in reality but which have persisted to this day.

The third class of heraldic books are those of the present century and many good ones have appeared. First of all, there is *Heraldry Explained* by the late A. C. Fox-Davies. This is a very good book and so is the author's larger work, *Complete Guide to Heraldry*. The former was unfortunately out of print for a time, but at the time of writing is being reprinted by David & Charles Ltd. of Newton Abbot, Devon. The larger book is published by Nelsons. Also produced by that company is Sir Iain Moncreiffe's *Simple Heraldry* to which reference has already been made. The books by Fox-Davies have one great fault, their author assumes that his theories are without any flaw. He knew little of the origin of Heraldry and was not prepared to admit any argument against his views. He was a barrister and thought in hard legalistic terms, up to a point, but his thinking seems largely to have been guided by the fact that his own arms were of fairly recent date.

Also very good are: *Intelligible Heraldry* by the brothers Sir Christopher and Adrian Lynch-Robinson. *Boutell's Heraldry* is good and has passed through many editions. *Heraldry in England* by Sir Anthony Wagner is a useful little book and has some very fine illustrations. It is a King Penguin.

On the score of illustrations you should get into the habit as soon as possible of seeing coats of arms in their full colours. It is not enough to study them in black and white because however good the drawings may be they cannot give you the full picture, unless colour is used. (See chapter 19).

Few writers have much to say about the history of Heraldry and it was because of this gap that I tried to write the Story of Heraldry in my book of that name first published in 1952 by *Country Life*, and now published by Charles Tuttle Co. Inc. of Tokyo, Japan & Vermont, U.S.A. Although it was written by myself I am compelled to mention it because no other history of Heraldry exists in English.

With regard to the Bayeux Tapestry the best book is by the

late Sir Eric Maclagan in the Penguin Books. In addition to the
evidence of the shields on the Tapestry as to the fact that
armorial bearings as such did not exist at the time of the
Norman Conquest, there is another item of proof. We have an
eye-witness account of the appearance of the Crusaders or
Frankish knights by Anna Comnena, the daughter of the
Emperor of Constantinople at the time of the First Crusade
(*circa* 1095). This lady was sufficiently remarkable in that at a
time when most of Europe was plunged in squalid ignorance,
she was a real historian and author of considerable note. In her
description of the Crusaders she says: "An additional weapon
of defence is a shield which is not round, but a long shield, very
broad, at the top and running out to a point, hollowed out
slightly inside, but externally smooth and gleaming with a
brilliant boss of molten brass." (*The Alexiad*, translated by
Elizabeth A. S. Dawes, 1928, page 341, Book XIII, c. VIII).
Had there been designs on the shields surely such a meticulous
writer would have mentioned them.

CHAPTER TWO

THE LANGUAGE OF HERALDRY

*The Anglo-French words and terms which are
used. The reason for the use of French in this
connection. The division into metals, colours and
furs.*

O NE of the puzzles which meets the student of Heraldry and
which has to be disposed of as quickly as may be is that of
the language. It seems very unfair that any reasonable man
should be exposed to language such as *three dexter buckles on a
sable ground gules* (this is the famous nonsense heraldic
description from John Galsworthy's *Forsyte Saga—Man of
Property*, Part Two, Chapter 7), but the difficulty vanishes
when one realizes that the language used is French, and old
French at that. Why French?

The French language was the first of the native tongues of
Europe to arrive at anything resembling an equality with
Latin. The latter had been of course the official language of
the Roman Empire, and Latin had gradually become the
everyday speech of people in Britain, France, Spain and other
western European countries as well as in Italy itself. When the
Roman Empire crashed, the civilization of Rome was over-
thrown in some countries, such as Britain in particular and
the invaders succeeded in destroying the Latin language in
daily use and substituting their own. But in France and Spain
the invaders were not strong enough to destroy all Latin
culture so that the Latin language lived on in a changed form,
apart from its use in the services of the Church or the daily
language of ecclesiastics. The French language, which was
derived from Latin, became a very fluent and powerful
medium of expression and by the end of the 12th century
French was the language in which the cultivated gentleman
expressed himself whether he were French, English, Scotch,
Sicilian, or even Palestinian by birth. It was a strange
accident which brought this to be true in England. The
Norman Conquest destroyed a great fabric of literature which

the invading Frenchmen for all their apparent brilliance could not match. The literature of the Old English ranged over every literary form since used by their descendants, poetry, drama, the novel, history, biography, philosophy, but the disaster of the Norman Conquest put the control of the country in the hands of French speakers. For 300 years the official languages of England were Latin and French until at last the loosening of the feudal system gave English once more its proper place.

It was only natural that if French should be the *lingua franca* of the worldly gentleman, just as Latin was of the churchman and the scholar, Heraldry would speak that language. About 1400 in England there was a movement to substitute English for old French terms, gold instead of or, silver instead of argent and so on, but this movement died out and the French terms are used to this day. This is not surprising. Norman French was used in the English Law Courts for pleading until about 1735, so that its present use in Heraldry is understandable.

Now as to the terms. A shield which is the main and essential constituent of any coat of arms may be of a certain number of colours, of metals or of furs. These are the three possible grounds of the shield, in other words they are the base of the shield. This base is called the field or ground. The derivation of these three classes is fairly straightforward. The colours are obviously those which were the earliest forms of differentiation between one shield and another. The metals are derived from the nature of a shield. The furs come from the rich drapings thrown or worn over the armour of richer knights.

All heraldic colours are vivid. There are no pastel shades in Heraldry. The colours are:

azure	i.e. blue
gules	red
purpure	purple
sable	black
vert	green

The metals are two:

argent	silver
or	gold.

Shields showing types of Fur.

The furs are four:

    ermine   white fur with black spots

    ermines i.e. black fur with white spots

    erminois   gold fur with black spots

    vair or vairé rows of small shields alternately reversed.

(There is also pean, another variant of ermine, black with gold ermine spots; and potent, a fur composed of T-shaped divisions.)

The rules of heraldry are that it is not right to put a colour upon a colour, a metal upon a metal or a fur upon a fur. That is one reason why the Forsyte arms are wrong, sable upon gules. There is one well-known exception to the rule about metals, that is in the case of the kingdom of Jerusalem, where the gold cross and crosses rest upon a silver ground.

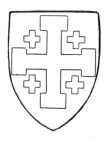

Arms of the City of
Jerusalem.

Now upon this basis of these three materials are built all the coats of arms which are used. The items which are put upon the ground are called charges. The shield is, shall we say, gules, and it is charged with whatever item is needed to differentiate it from others. The trouble about charges is that as the number of coats of arms multiplies the need to difference them as it is termed in Heraldry grows ever greater. For instance suppose two persons of the name of Pine, but having as far as they can see no connection; both use arms or wish to use arms with the natural play upon the name, of a pine tree, pine cone, pine apple. They cannot both use the same coat of arms unless they are blood relations. Their arms must be differenced, usually in favour of the older coat. Thus the pine tree in the crest may be encircled with a ducal coronet to distinguish the owner's arms from those of the older line. In the case of William Shakespeare as no coat armour existed for his family the heralds of Queen Elizabeth I's time gave him a spear in his arms as an obvious play upon his name. The present Sir Geoffrey Shakespeare, whose family is of Warwickshire has the spear also but with certain difference marks in the rest of the shield to show that no blood connection with the family of the dramatist is intended, though such may exist.

John Shakespeare,
Stratford-on-Avon, 1596.

(For puns upon names and words in Heraldry see the next chapter. It is called canting).

The original shields were much simpler than those of to-day because there were fewer of them and therefore the need to differentiate did not arise so frequently. As we shall see in chapter 5, it was possible for several families to use the same coat of arms though they had no blood connection with each other. The need for difference marks grows greater each year. The number of coats of arms now in existence probably runs into 100,000 in the British Isles alone. In *Burke's General Armory* which was last published in 1878* there are 60,000 and many more have been created since then in addition to those which Burke could not find but which research has since brought to light.

The early charges were such things as bends, chevrons,

*The *Armory* has been reprinted since but not edited.

chiefs, piles, fesses, bars, and crosses. These charges would naturally suggest themselves to the early users. *Azure a bend or.* Blue with a gold bend across it. This was a very easy design for a coat of arms.

Two misunderstandings need to be removed. There is nothing in Heraldry which suggests that a bend sinister is the necessary sign of bastardy. There are ways of denoting bastardy; in England it is often done by debruising the arms of the father with a baton on the sinister, or by surrounding the arms with a bordure. The latter is the favourite method in Scotland. Sinister has nothing to do with underhanded dealing. Sinister is used in heralds' language in its Latin sense of left, while dexter is right. It must be remembered that a shield as we look at it is the reverse from its position for the holder. All shields were originally in actual use and so what appears to us to be the right side is really the sinister, and vice versa. A bend sinister is merely a bend across the shield from left to right. Why it is used in literature and in journalism for a token of bastardy is one of the minor mysteries.

Another common misunderstanding is that for every name there exists a crest or coat of arms. This is a delusion. There are many names for which no coat of arms can be found anywhere, for the simple reason that the bearers of the name have never been armigerous. On the other hand it would be a gross error to assume that where a name is common there are no armigerous honours associated with it. There are many coats of arms for Brown, Smith, Jones, Robinson, etc.

Note: Arms of Jerusalem. There are other instances similar to that of Jerusalem, but the practice is not used in modern heraldry.

CHAPTER THREE

THE MAKE-UP OF THE COAT OF ARMS

or armorial achievement. The shield, crest, mantling, supporters, helmet, motto and the charges on the shield.

THE shield as already explained is the essential part of the coat of arms or achievement. Without the shield there cannot be a coat of arms. The shape of the shield may vary just as the design of the arms as a whole may vary and in fact does. A book such as *Burke's Peerage* which has within its pages examples of the heraldic art produced in several generations is in some respects like a museum or art gallery. It would be possible to have half a dozen examples of the same coat of arms yet to the uninitiated it would appear that they were different coats. The reason for this is that the artists in making up their designs have been influenced as all artists are by varying fashions and styles in Heraldry. The coat of arms in these varying styles is essentially the same but in the course of years the artistic style altered. So with the shield it may be shown as square, as curved, as hanging slant-wise, and so on. Many people have a decided objection to the slant-wise shield though this style is in fact more like that of the mediaeval period and is used a good deal by the artists of the College of Arms. Another point which the beginner needs to have in mind is that objects in Heraldry are not necessarily depicted in the same form as in their natural state. An heraldic tiger is not the same thing by any means as the native of the Indian jungle. So much is this the case that when it became necessary to bring the real tiger into heraldry in connection with the arms of persons who had achieved fame in the Indian Empire, the new creation, for such it was, was always referred to as a Bengal tiger. There are in Heraldry many fictitious animals such as the wyvern, the griffin and the dragon; in many cases in modern arms grants, the recipient cannot understand the pained horror which the heraldic artist feels at being told to go to the zoo to see what a kangaroo or a wallaby, a rhinoceros or a giraffe looks like. The heraldic is like the surrealist artist in this respect, he has the desire to dominate his art, and not to be merely photographic.

From the shield we come to the helmet. This object exemplifies the essentially practical side of original Heraldry. In the days when knights were bold, and armigerous, everyone wore a helmet of some sort in battle, so everyone now is entitled to a helmet in his grant of arms. Heraldry has shown a power of adaptation which has enabled it to live when other contemporary arts such as armour making died out, but it still retains its nexus with the remote past. Hence the helmet borne by the newly ennobled city magnate or the grocer who has made good. The shape of the helmet is like that of the shield, varied. Some helmets are those of the tilting variety, which have eye-space hardly sufficient it would seem for a man to have any sort of view. Others are the barrel type where the weight began to rest on the shoulders. More important than the shape of the helmet is its position. In the older days of Heraldry the position of the helmet in the coat of arms varied as much as the shape of helmets, but since the 17th century there have been rules laid down and generally observed for the delineation of helmets. A royal helmet is of gold, placed affrontée, i.e. with the helmet full face on, and the bars of the helmet down but the visor piece raised. The helmet of a peer is silver, in profile, visor raised and the bars of gold. The helmet of a baronet or knight is steel, affrontée, visor up and without bars or grills. The helmet of an esquire or gentleman is steel, in profile, visor closed.

The wreath is the means of fastening the crest to the helmet. When an artist depicts a shield with the crest above it on the wreath but the latter not attached to the helmet, he is guilty of an heraldic solecism. The crest cannot be airborne as though independent of the rest of the achievement. The wreath was of silk with a cord twisted round it and the crest was fastened on it. The modern practice is to show the wreath in the alternate colours of the shield. In the case of peers a chapeau or cap of maintenance is used in place of the wreath to hold the crest, the reason for this being that a peer is entitled to a chapeau when in official robes. However, the usage of chapeaux spread from the peers to persons who were not peers and many grants of chapeaux took place at one time although the recipients had no connection with the peerage. Crest coronets are also found, where the crest rests upon a coronet somewhat similar to that of a peer.

The crest itself is perhaps the commonest known of all the parts of a coat of arms, for it has usurped the name applicable

Arms of D'Arcy showing Chapeau Couché Shield and Bouche in dexter chief.

to the whole achievement. Crests were very rudimentary things at one time, probably made of leather or light wood. The wonderful crests of modern times would have been out of place in mediaeval warfare. One Burmese knight had a Chinese pagoda as his crest. In other cases there are sailing ships in full sail as crests and all sorts of weird bearings. The origin of the crest is not easy to determine, but there is something to be said for the idea that it came from the sport of the tournament. The latter was an expensive business and only the greater families could go in for it. The loser had to give up his armour and horse to the victor. In one case, that of Prince Edward, later King Edward I, he was only able to participate in a tournament when his mother pawned some of her jewels to pay for his equipment. As he was defeated in the pastime, one wonders what were the reactions of his parent. The so-called tournament rank families did not exist as such in this country, though they did on the Continent. In Germany there was a ceremony known as the *Helm Schau* when the squires of the knights carried their masters' helmets on display so that all could see the crests. But in Britain as abroad only the wealthy families could afford the tournament so that at first, only the great families have crests. In the 16th and 17th centuries it became the fashion for the Heralds in their Visitations (see chapter 8) to grant crests to families which bore arms but had hitherto had no such addition to their coats. In many cases arms are allowed in one Visitation and the crest in another some 50 years later. Very probably the crest had been in the meantime assumed by the family, following that well-known principle in English life which makes it imperative for the Jones to have a cocktail cabinet or a larger car if the Smiths next door possess these things. There are few families to-day who possess arms without a crest. Some like the Churchills of Muston have no crest and for this reason we can be sure both of the antiquity of the family and of its arms; but no grant to-day would be made of arms without a crest. Curiously enough there is one case on record at the College of Arms in which the crest was granted without the full coat of arms. The reason was that the grantee of the arms when shown the proposed arms in draft did not like the shield but agreed to the crest. The crest was accordingly entered in the College books but the shield was respited for further consideration. Meantime the grantee died, so that his is the only case known of a grant of a crest with nothing else. (See note at end of chapter). The use of the crest illustrates the spread of Heraldry among classes such as the

C

richer merchants of the Tudor period, as among the upper middle classes in the late 18th century and 19th century, of ideas which had formerly been the exclusive concern of the landed or knightly families. The use of the crest (usually with motto) on objects such as spoons or nowadays on motor cars where the full coat of arms cannot be easily depicted has had a great deal to do with the employment of the term "crest" for the whole coat of arms. *Burke's General Armory* did much to cause the use of the crest alone. In Victorian times the heraldic stationer flourished mightily. When a gentleman ordered his stationery, it was easy for the stationer to ask, "Will you have your crest on the paper, sir?" and if the customer hesitated, for him to turn up the arms in the *Armory*. The practice became so general that it was quite usual for certain firms to advertise that they would engrave signets or stamp notepaper with crests, given the customer's name and address, his county of origin, and 3s. 6d. The vogue of crests on notepaper had a long run and was only just going out when I first, in 1935, became conversant with the editing of Burke. Apart from the *General Armory*, a special book was written to advise those who sought crests. This was *Fairbairn's Book of Crests*, a work which is now again in print. It is a well-illustrated book but of little use to the real student of Heraldry because it is in the worst form of truncated heraldry, giving only family names, and the drawing of the crest. One of the establishments which dealt in family crests was situated at Lincoln's Inn Turnstile and not long ago when I saw the building being demolished, I gave a last look at the bold signs "Armorial Ensigns Engraved Etc." which had given pleasure to so many in a more civilised age.

As to the form of crests, the original crests when used in war must have been fairly light. In the tournament the crest was often made of leather and could become heavy, but as it was worn only during a few courses in tilting its weight did not overcome the wearer. In battle when a whole day might have to be passed in armour the crest was lighter and was made of a thin plate of metal. In fact the crest may have developed from a comb-like arrangement on the back of the helmet. This appears in many German examples. In manuscript scenes too one often sees plumes on top of the helmet, a custom known in many ages, but not a crest. Thus in real warfare the crest tended to be simple, a dragon for the Earl of Lancaster, a lion for the Earl of Nottingham. But as it ceased to be used in warfare it became more and more an object which could not have been so employed. A stag on a block of stone, a ship of the line in full sail, these are typical of the curious and unheraldic crests which have appeared in modern heraldry. Other cases which can be quoted are (Glasford) *two hands issuing from clouds and grasping a rod and having between them a horn of plenty*. Or (Samuel) *a wolf upon a rock with three spears behind it*. These things could never have been used in the days of chivalry.

The next item to be described is the lambrequin or mantling. This is the flowing drapery arrangement which can be seen in most drawings of arms depending from the helmet and flowing around the whole achievement. The origin of the mantling is again like most things in Heraldry very practical. In the burning heat of the East when the Crusades were fought the helmet became very hot and tiring and the mantling began like the old covering for the back of the neck which was used for many generations by British soldiers in the East (until the last war when medical science found out that a man stripped to the waist and hatless could fight and live through the heats of India and Burma). It was extended so as to cover great parts of the armour and it was found useful not only in keeping off the heat but in catching the sword points of opponents. Hence the jagged edges sometimes seen in mantling. The colours of the mantling are (nowadays) the two main colours of the shield. In the case of peers it was formerly the custom to show their arms upon a background of the robe of estate which was worn on great occasions by noblemen. In Europe the background of the arms for sovereigns was the pavilion, a tent-like object which had the arms shown within it. The ermine mantle forms the background of the arms of many Continental nobility.

Supporters are perhaps among the most familiar heraldic objects. Most people have seen the supporters of the royal arms, and those of many corporate arms are well known. Supporters are those figures on either side of the coat of arms which hold the shield and do appear to support it. It is thought that they originated from the desire of artists and engravers to show the shield actually upheld by something, and to fill in spaces in the area round the arms drawing. To-day the use of supporters is rigidly controlled, and in England their use is confined to peers, to Knights of the Garter, the Thistle, St. Patrick, and to Knights Grand Cross and Knights Grand Commander of other Orders such as that of the British Empire, also in a very few cases to persons whose merits have brought them into great renown. Among families of English gentry one sometimes comes across instances of the use of supporters which have been derived from the past. The Fountaines of Narford in Norfolk have supporters which are often shown with their arms. The reason is that they were granted to a collateral ancestor of the family, Sir Andrew Fountaine, Warden of the Mint after Sir Isaac Newton, in 1727. For various services he received a grant of supporters to his arms. Another case is that of Chetwynd Stapylton, a family which has almost invariably borne supporters to its arms since the 17th century. The family pedigree rolls show the arms of Sir Miles Stapleton who flourished about 1660 with two talbots (i.e. dogs) argent as supporters, and in Whighill church in Yorkshire where the family formerly owned property, there is a monument to Robert Stapilton (who died 11 March 1635) with the same two supporters. Sir William Dugdale in his *Visitations of Yorkshire* refers to the supporters of the Stapyltons. Whatever their origin they seem to have been generally in use in these two instances for some centuries. With Speke of Jordan, the supporters usually shown are those of one member of the family, William Speke, to whom they were granted for life, in memory of his son, the discoverer of the sources of the Nile, to whom a memorial exists in Kensington Gardens. This grant was definitely for the life of the grantee only, so the supporters cannot, as in the other cases quoted, descend to the rest of the family.

In Scotland the use of supporters is much wider. Scottish Heraldry as will be seen later is on a different basis from English. Not only peers but also private gentlemen of ancient lineage may often be entitled to supporters on the ground of long usage. Also the families of the lesser barons, who in England are found more among the squirearchy, are often granted supporters by the Lord Lyon. Thus a family of Grahame of Morphie, which is not now counted among titled families, had supporters for the head of the family, and this is often the case among the great Scottish untitled families.

The motto is the subject of much confusion among popular writers. There are countless references to family mottoes in

Arms of Chetwynd-Stapleton, showing supporters.

romance and we are usually told that the motto originated at some remote period of the family history, and had a definite allusion to the family fortunes or to family character, or in some way meant a great deal. It is true that some mottoes must have originated in this way, and some even as war cries, like the *Crom-a boo* of the Fitzgeralds; in most cases mottoes are of late adoption, are quite unsuitable for war cries, and have no more historic allusion than any other respectable matter within a particular family.

There are some curious mottoes, like that of Martin: *He that looks at Martin's ape Martin's ape shall look at him*, or that of the Murrays, Aynsleys and Stewarts, *Furth fortune and fill the fetters*, which are quite obviously reminiscent of ages past but the meaning of which has long been forgotten. Mottoes are not part of a coat of arms though they often appear painted beneath the arms, but they are much quoted among the descriptions of arms and thus an impression has grown up that they form part of the arms. Mottoes are not hereditary, they can be changed at the will of the owner and are purely arbitrary. In Scotland they are usually shown above the crest, in England below the whole shield.

Having thus dealt with the different components of the coat of arms we can now go on to the ordinaries or charges which are shown on the grounds of the shield, as enumerated in chapter 2. To describe a shield in heraldic language is to blazon it. To paint it is to trick it. The rules of blazoning are fairly straightforward, and can be summarised thus. First the field must be described, whether it is a colour, a metal or a fur. Thus the field is or, gold. On this there will be a charge, say a chevron. The description is then *or a chevron gules*. But such a simple description is unlikely. The chevron may be marked in some way. Thus, *Or a chevron gules thereon two wolves' heads argent*. But there may be other charges on the shield, say, three pickaxes. *Or a chevron gules thereon two wolves' heads argent between three pickaxes gules*.

There are various ordinaries as they are called which are used as primary charges and these ordinaries often assume a form of lines of a quasi mathematical nature. Such are the bend, the pale, the fesse, chevron, pile, cross (in the last case there are said to be 400 examples, though only about 20 are in regular use), the saltire, the quarter, canton, inescutcheon, bordure, lozenge, flaunch, roundel, fret, label, billet, etc. (See Glossary for meanings of individual terms). Then after these come the charges as they are called which are usually of an animal nature or of some other actual object found in daily life. The reason for the use of animals in Heraldry goes back far behind heraldic matters and relates to the identification of himself with the animals to which man has always been prone. The curious natural history of the Middle Ages, undisturbed by any contact with nature is responsible for most of the charges used in Heraldry. The writers on Heraldry to whom I have already referred, such as Guillim and Edmondson, give numerous instances of a doctrine of the meaning of the symbols in Heraldry which has no foundation in fact. The pelican does not nourish its young with its own blood (from this belief comes its use in Heraldry as a symbol of Christ or God), the toad has not a jewel in its head, the snake is not necessarily a possessor of wisdom, the salamander does not live unconsumed in the midst of flame, and so on. The natural history of mediaeval times was based upon the interpretation of books and was not bothered by awkward facts derived from the study of nature, out in the woods and streams, and from this fabulous natural history the Heraldry of the period is derived and is with us still.

Among the more familiar charges in Heraldry will be found beasts, especially beasts of prey like the lion and leopard; monsters, such as the wyvern, griffin, dragon, etc.; birds; reptiles; insects; trees, fruits; and into modern times many inanimate objects such as aeroplanes (the charge occurs in the arms of the borough of Wallington); ships (in the arms of Fulham); rolls of parchment (for a newspaper magnate), and almost every variety of objects to be found in real life.

Note: According to Fox-Davies, *Complete Guide to Heraldry*, page 337, the person who received a crest without the rest of the arms was a member of the family of Buckworth.

CHAPTER FOUR

THE LANGUAGE OF SYMBOLISM

*in western Heraldry, instances of a play on
words (canting Heraldry) and cases in which
the origin of the charges can be traced.*

IT has already been mentioned in the last chapter that
Heraldry has used a language supposed to have symbolic
meaning but this meaning existed mainly in the imagination of
16th and 17th century writers. This symbolism was the product of the natural history of the Middle Ages which sprang
from a too-reliant study of the works of Aristotle and Pliny
through the medium often of bad translations and uncertain
texts and which produced views that would mightily have
amused those great authors. Only occasionally can the origin of
a charge on a coat of arms be traced. One instance in which the
true original meaning can be deduced is that of the arms of
Lord Stourton. The description of these arms is: *Sable a bend
or between six fountains proper.* The fountain of Heraldry is
not like a real fountain. There is a charge known as a roundel,
a plain circular figure. An heraldic fountain is a roundel
described as *barry wavy argent and azure.* The fountains can
be seen in the illustration of Stourton. The name Stourton is a
territorial surname, derived from the place name where the
family had their property, which is situated in Wiltshire. The
manor of Stourton derives its name from the River Stour and
the source of the latter is the six wells found in Stourton Park.
Guillim remarks that these six fountains in the Stourton arms
are borne to signify six springs, from which the river Stour has
its beginnings. Three of the springs were inside the park and
three outside and we see that in the coat of arms the six
fountains are divided into equal numbers by the bend. Here
then is an explanation of an old coat of arms, but such
explanations are rare. The origin of many of the oldest heraldic
charges which are known is lost in the times when no writer
had thought of putting down notes about such matters. The
explanation of the name Buccleuch "when in the cleuch the

buck was ta'en'', or of Naesmith as the explanation of the blacksmith who was in reality an indignant nobleman compelled to disguise his identity, are no more fanciful—and no more truthful—than the derivations given for coats of arms. Where we are able to trace the meaning it can be seen that the origin is not something grand and heroic, or supernatural, but quite prosaic and ordinary. The family of Gorges, one of

Arms of Stourton symbolising the River Stour and the
six springs or "Fountains" in Stourton Park
which are its source.

the greatest in mediaeval history, bears a whirlpool in its arms. The reason is a play on the name. Gorges in Latin is gurges, which means a whirlpool. In the case of the Davenports, the crest of the family is a man's (some versions say a felon's) head, with a rope about its neck. The explanation here is probably that in old days the Davenports had the office of catching and executing robbers. The ancient families of Pilkington and Trafford have similar crests: Pilkington has a mower with a scythe and Trafford has a mower with a flail. The mottoes are:

Now thus. The legend is that the Pilkingtons or Traffords of the Norman Conquest period were doing their best to impede the Norman Conquerors but that being surprised by over-whelming odds on one occasion the representative of the family took refuge in a barn as a thresher and when asked questions pretended to be an idiot who had no more to say than "Now thus". It is of course quite impossible to say whether there is any truth in this story. There must have been much opposition to the Normans especially in the rougher parts of the country but few stories except that of Hereward the Wake have been preserved. One legend regarding a Scottish coat is worth quoting. The McKies have in their arms two ravens pierced by the same arrow. The family legend is that when Robert Bruce was in hiding with a peasant family one of the sons discovered his identity and showed his skill to the king by transfixing two ravens with the same arrow. I have heard it added by one of the McKies, that the original McKie was the unknown friend of Bruce mentioned in Barbour's account of Bruce's wanderings when in disguise!

Gurges for Gorges.

The arms of Gorges are an example of what is called canting Heraldry. This means that the charge in the shield is a pun on the name of the owner of the arms. Thus a Weir will very probably find a fish weir in his arms. Crook will have a shepherd's crook, Buckland a buck on a rock. Some puns are lost to us because of changes in language. The Geddes bear fish in their arms, because a ged was the name for certain fishes.

Lucy also bears fish because the luce is the old name of a fish. Trumpington had two trumpets, Septvans had seven winnowing fans. The practice of canting or punning upon the arms bearer's name is deep-rooted in Heraldry and is not likely to

Arms of Lord Crook of Carshalton: Granted 1947

pass away. It is too obviously useful in making up the charges in a coat of arms, especially in the case of institutions.

Heads in Heraldry would have a fascinating story to tell if only we could get at all the facts. The Moor's head or the Saracen's head is bound to be claimed as derived from a Crusading ancestor by any family which owns such crest. Some Welsh families bear Englishmen's heads in their arms. The

Lloyds of Denbigh have three Englishmen's heads in their shield. This commemorates a defeat inflicted upon the hated Saxons. The Lloyds of Plymog have an Englishman's head as crest. Here is a definite historical allusion but in the great majority of cases we cannot pierce the mists of time. The meaning of charges is for ever lost to us. I have often wondered what legend lies behind the simple motto, *I saved the King*, of the Torrance family.* One of the most necessary lessons in Heraldry which needs to be reiterated again and again is that family legends of great deeds whereby shields were won or additions made to the existing arms are not worth repeating and must be resolutely abandoned even if they exist in one's own family. This is a hard saying but unless the student is prepared to strip away at the outset the crust of fiction which has gathered over the realities of Heraldry he or she will make little progress.

There is a school of writers, principally in Latin countries, which believes that totemism is at the base of heraldic symbols. There may be something in this and as the theory is presented with much learning it cannot but be sympathetically considered. The reasoning of this school, of which we shall have more to say in chapter 16, depends upon certain undoubted facts, the use of symbols in all ages, and the belief of ancient man that he was descended from the higher animals, namely those which he so much admired. The totem system of the Indians of North America shows this belief in full force. The guardian spirit of the tribe is envisaged as in the form of an animal. Many examples are found in the monumental work, Frazer's *Golden Bough*. One example is quoted from the life of the Ainu tribes, the aborigines of Japan. The Ainu keep or kept a bear to which they paid great homage and addressed as a father, but which in the end they slew ceremonially. The theory is that among the primitive symbols used by man, there were found totems from which Heraldry derived, because in their infancy all the peoples of the world believed that they descended from animals, animals which are seen to-day in the

* From a correspondent I have been informed that Robert the Bruce was the King, and one of the Torrance family saved him. I cannot vouch, of course, for this. The arms of Torrance as given in *Burke's General Armory* are: *per pale gules and or, two boat oars in saltire azure. Crest—a bull's head erased.*

shields of arms, as eagles, bulls, lions, leopards, serpents, doves, dogs, horses and many others. In addition there are chimerical figures of mythical animals. The man at arms showed himself proud of the totemic symbol of his predecessor or ancestor, the protector of the tribe, clan or group, whose qualities of valour, tenacity, and wisdom he desired to emulate. There seems little doubt that this may account for the great use of animal figures in Heraldry.

Another subject closely connected with the use of symbols and the meaning of the latter is that of augmentations. Alongside the legend that someone was granted a coat of arms for some achievement or characteristic, goes the story that something in the family arms was a reward for service done. A legend which circulates sometimes in books, even in a few which emanate from the College of Arms is that the canton in the top righthand of some shields is a reward for service done by esquires. As no records exist of such service ever having been performed there is not much point in circulating such a story.

Most of the genuine augmentations are well known. An augmentation is an addition to a coat of arms made at the command of the Sovereign. Instances of many such augmentations can be found in most heraldic works. One of the best examples is taken from the Victorian era. The arms of Viscount Gough contain more than one augmentation. This general distinguished himself in various engagements in the Peninsular War, in China and in India where he fought against the Sikhs. The results of his military career can be read in the description of his arms which occupies thirty lines of small type in *Burke's Peerage*. The family crest and arms are almost obliterated in this description and one has to struggle to find out what they are. One of the earlier augmentations shows the wall of a city breached (the city being Tarifa), but lest there should be too many empty places in the shield, a representation is added of the badge of the Spanish Order of Charles III. The wall of Tarifa is the eastern wall. The badge of Charles III is dependent from a ribbon and minute details are given of the colour and form of the ribbon. The result is a very ugly piece of work. An even worse example of a genuine augmentation is found, however, in the arms of Ross. The achievements of an ancestor were commemorated by charging the top of the shield (called

the fesse) with a portion of the terrestrial globe. The globe is to
be depicted with the position of the meridian, the Arctic Circle,
etc.; there are two crests, one of which is a rock with a flagstaff
flying the Union Jack inscribed with the date, June 1, 1831,
when the magnetic pole was discovered by Sir John Ross, who

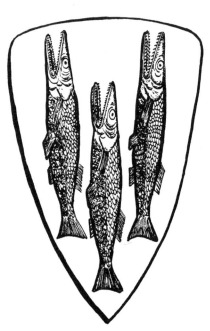

Arms of Lucy: early example of canting arms
(also early shield type).

also endeavoured to find the lost explorer Franklin. There are
other details in the arms and crest of Ross which obviously
could never have been dreamed of in ancient Heraldry. On the
other hand the augmentation of the Duke of Wellington was
fairly simple, consisting of the crosses of St. George, St.
Andrew and St. Patrick, and these were shown on an

inescutcheon, that is a small shield set in the midst of the coat of arms or shield.

Among examples of allusive arms may be mentioned those of Lord Beaverbrook, where there are two maple leaves in the chief, a thistle in the base, emblems which are reminiscent of his Scottish Canadian origin. His supporters are beavers, and two barrulets (or small bars) are in the shield as being reminiscent of waves. The Harmsworth family has an allusion to its origin in the two rolls of paper joined in saltire (i.e. St. Andrew's Cross style) between four flying bees. The crest of the Harmsworths is a cubit arm which holds a roll of paper.

Other cases of heraldic allusion bear reference to a man's occupation. For Lord Joicey, three sable lozenges and two miners' picks are evidence of the family's connection with the coal mining industry. The family of Herschel, baronets, has a 40-foot reflecting telescope in its shield and the symbol of Uranus in the top of the shield which Sir William Herschel, the founder of the family, discovered. This is well in the tradition of such arms as those of Lucy where three luces (or fishes) are shown. Sir Thomas Lucy was the man to whom was traditionally attributed the trial and punishment of Shakespeare for deer stealing. Lord Calverley's arms show some reference to his career, a golden fleece (that being a sheep suspended) recalling his employment as a textile worker (this refers to the first Lord Calverley); the two miners' picks crossed in saltire before a miner's lamp are a reminder of his natural piety (in the Virgilian sense) his father having been a miner.

CHAPTER FIVE

THE DEVELOPMENT OF HERALDRY
IN WESTERN EUROPE

*Were arms invented for themselves by the
original users or were they granted? The
earliest written evidence. Rolls of Arms.*

L ONG before the appearance of John of Guildford's *Tractatus de Armis* in about 1394, there were the Rolls of Arms
to which I have already referred. About 60 years after the time
of Richard Coeur de Lion, we have the first of the English Rolls
of Arms. Before there was anything resembling a Heralds'
College in England or elsewhere in Europe, collections of arms
had been written down in various forms, sometimes by heralds
who were interested in making such collections, sometimes by
scribes and recorders who found the Rolls useful in aiding their
memories at tournaments and other official musters of nobles
and knights. England is especially rich in these Rolls. It was a
Scot, the late J. Storer Clouston, who wrote: "The good
fortune of England in preserving so much of her past is
nowhere more conspicuous than in her great collections of
heraldic Rolls or lists of nobles, knights and squires, with the
arms they anciently bore, from the middle of the 13th century
onwards. Ours in Scotland begin so comparatively late as the
16th century, and there is very little of definitely certain date
then, till one reaches the 1540s." (*Proceedings of the Soc. of
Antiquaries of Scotland*, 10 Jan. 1938). Particulars are available of 100 major Rolls in England, which date from 1250 to
the early 1500s, just before the beginning of the Heralds'
Visitations. It is to the wars with Scotland that we owe several
early heraldic Rolls. The Falkirk Roll gives the arms of those
who served under Edward I at Falkirk in 1298. The arms of
111 persons are described in this Roll. They are divided into
those whose banners were in the vanguard, or in one of the four
"battles" into which the army at Falkirk was divided. Thus the
arms were borne on the banners of these outstanding persons,

and as we let our mind's eye roam over the list we can picture a scene of great awe and beauty as the vanguard and the four succeeding lines of battle approached the narrow plain where the Scots were waiting for them. The banners made a fine sight as their colours stood out against the steel harness of the knights and the darker leather jerkins of the less heavily armoured footmen. Many of the most famous names in England appear in this list: Percy of Northumberland, Wake of Lincolnshire, Fitzwilliam, Hastings, Moulton, Despenser, Clifford, Basset, and De Vere, Earl of Oxford. Another very interesting Roll dates from the reign of Edward II, and is known as The Great Parliamentary or Bannerets Roll, from about 1312. It contains the names and arms of 1,120 persons. The division is by counties. One of the most fascinating of all the Rolls is that of the *Siege of Caerlaverock*. It is written in Norman French and relates the siege and capture in 36 hours of a small castle in Dumfriesshire in the year 1300 during the July campaign of that year in Scotland by King Edward I. There is much more in the poem than a roll of arms. The poet describes the mediaeval method of siege making which would seem to have been at this time at least, very unsoldierly and costly. The knights and men-at-arms assaulted the castle pell-mell and not unnaturally received the full dint of the defenders' stones and dislodged masonry. The description of the assault is reminiscent of *Ivanhoe*. Of Richard de Kirkbride the poet says, "so stoutly was the gate of the castle assailed by him, that never did smith with his hammer strike his iron as he and his did there." Surely we can hear the Black Knight wielding his axe against the gate of Torquilstone; and many an archer's feat in romance must have been based on the incident in the poem when a Scot who displays a flag of truce has his hand pierced through to his face by an arrow. The author's main purpose was of course to describe the arms of those present at the siege. He describes some 87 banners and 106 coats of arms (usually banner and shield bore the same arms). It has been conjectured that the author was a herald in the train of King Edward. He may have been, we do not know. Whoever he was, he was a bold man, for in describing the bearers of arms he gives pen pictures, which are not always flattering, of their characters. The Roll shows that the science of Heraldry after 150 years of existence was in perfect shape. It was a useful science because of its value in war; snobbery did not enter into it. The management of the charges borne on the shield was perfectly carried out. It had to be, or heraldic devices would not have fulfilled their function. But the warriors who used these devices were wont to arrange their armorial differences among themselves without recourse to king or heralds. Thus at Caerlaverock, Brian FitzAlan bore: *Barry or and gules*, which was, says the poet, the subject of a dispute between him and Hugh Pointz, who bore the same neither more nor less, at which many marvelled. Other instances of the irregular—as it would now be thought by many—uses of arms are given in the poem. Ralph de Monthermer, who was of obscure origin, had married Joan, daughter of Edward I, and in right of his wife had acquired the earldoms of Gloucester and Hereford. At the siege Ralph bore a banner with the arms of Clare (his wife's first husband's arms) *or three chevronels gules*. He bore on his shield his own arms, *or an eagle displayed vert*. John de Cromwell used his own arms, *azure a lion rampant double queued* (i.e. double tailed) *argent, crowned or*, but from other manuscripts we know that he used on occasions the arms of the house of Vipoint, *gules, six annulets or*, because his wife was an heiress of that family.

We can deduce various theories from these Rolls as to the way in which arms came to be adopted, and the case of FitzAlan and Pointz is indicative of the truth that the same arms were assumed by totally unrelated persons. Fortunately we do not have to rely only on inferences, for we have a famous case some two generations after Caerlaverock, that of *Scrope v. Grosvenor*, which is a leading case in matters heraldic. Really the case is that of *Scrope v. Grosvenor and Carminow*, for in fact there were three men, not related by blood, who all used the same coat of arms, *azure a bend or* Carminow from Cornwall, Grosvenor from Cheshire, Scrope from Yorkshire, all flourished in the reigns of Edward III and Richard II, and all bore the simple coat, the blue field with the golden bend. The arms had obviously been assumed at some time by the ancestors of the three men, no doubt because they were simple and easy for use. The three persons lived in different parts of England and did not come into contact with each other until they joined the King's army for the campaigns of France and Scotland.

Scrope was a great noble, and it must have galled him to see his arms borne by persons of inferior social status who were not related to him. But Carminow was a Cornishman, and no consideration of mere rank could weigh with him. Taking the initiative, he challenged Scrope's right to the arms. When the case was heard by the Court of Chivalry (see chapter 9), Scrope produced the pedigree of his undoubtedly ancient lineage. Like many or most of the nobles of his day, he claimed Norman ancestry. The legend of the Norman Conquest had already gripped the imagination of the proud knights of England. But to the Cornishman, as to most Celts, it meant very little. He traced his ancestry, he said, from the time of King Arthur, when his family had borne *azure a bend or*. The Court of Chivalry was duly impressed and embarrassed. The romances which were one of the staple entertainments of courtly society all spoke of Arthur and his knights, and as mediaeval writers were accustomed to clothe the past in garments of their own day, naturally the Arthurian figures were assumed to have had coat armour. Cornwall had always been King Arthur's county, and the bold Cornishman refused to lower his shield to any nobleman. Eventually a compromise was reached, Carminow kept his paternal arms though he was supposed to difference them with a canton. The reasoning of the Court was that he would return to Cornwall after the campaign and Scrope would not encounter his opposition any more. The family of Carminow continued as landed gentry until the 17th century and as they are still represented among living families in the female line the quartering of *azure a bend or* is still apparent in such sources as *Burke's Landed Gentry*. In the meantime the Scropes and Carminows continued to bear the same arms although they were not related. Why not? The arms had clearly never been granted by anyone but assumed on the authority of the individuals who adopted them. One of the great heraldic authorities of the period, Bartholus, a great name in international law (see next chapter), remarked that arms were like names, and could be assumed as a person pleased.

The proceedings between Scrope and Grosvenor were much more serious, and as the families in both cases exist at the present day in the male line, the matter is the more important.

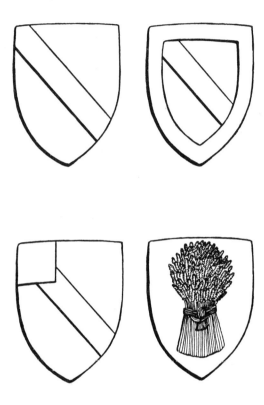

Scrope, Grosvenor (suggested), Carminow, Grosvenor
(adopted).

The case lasted for five years, a truly English Royal Commission! The witnesses were numerous and their evidence was recorded in two large volumes. Sir Robert Grosvenor the defendant in the case was a Cheshire knight of good family but not of great wealth. Lord Scrope was one of the wealthiest and most powerful nobles of the day, and one of his relatives is referred to by Shakespeare as holding the realm in fee. Many influential witnesses appeared on behalf of Scrope, including the poet Geoffrey Chaucer. In good faith Sir Robert Grosvenor claimed that his ancestors had used the disputed arms since the Norman Conquest and from the muniment chest of his landlord the Abbot of Vale Royal, he produced lists of knightly Grosvenors of whose existence unfortunately modern genealogists have been unable to find any proof. In the end the Court of Chivalry offered Grosvenor a variant of the Scrope arms, the addition of a wavy bordure argent (i.e. a wavy line running round inside the outline of the shield) but he refused to accept this and appealed to the Crown, in the person of Richard II. It may be noted that from the Court of Chivalry appeal lies only to the Crown. That erratic if artistic monarch, Richard II, gave his decision quickly. Sir Robert Grosvenor must give up the arms, which were to be reckoned as peculiarly Scrope's, and must pay the costs of the action. The decision is often cited as an instance of the control, in the last resort, exercised by the Crown over the right to bear arms. If so it appears to be entirely arbitrary. While Grosvenor was condemned, Carminow's family continued with the arms now supposed to be adjudged as Scrope's. Furthermore, Grosvenor, although forced by the King to give up his coat of arms, promptly consoled himself by assuming another coat—*azure a garb* (i.e. a sheaf of corn) *or*, ever since borne by his descendants. In passing we may note that the Scropes have long since ceased to be in the Peerage and are now simply squires in Yorkshire, whereas the Grosvenors have steadily mounted in the social scale and are now represented by the Dukes of Westminster. Both the late Duke and Mr. Scrope of Danby were Vice-Presidents of the Heraldry Society.

Before leaving the subject, we may note that Lord Scrope was appointed in 1395 a commissioner to determine a dispute as to the right to bear the arms—*gules three chevronels or* (chevronels are small versions of the chevron, similar to an inverted stripe of an N.C.O.)—on the part of Thomas Baude and Nicholas de Singleton, strangers in blood to each other. In this case the King issued a command to several nobles to settle the case. It would appear that there were many instances of the same arms being used by different persons. (Also in the French wars, another Scrope, Sir William, found a captured French knight, the Sieur Philippe de la Moustre wearing the same arms). Gradually the royal control over arms as over titles grew until in the 17th century it was rejected, and has only been gradually and not entirely revived effectually in our own time. We may now, however, profitably look at some of the writers on Heraldry in the earliest days. After all they were there when arms were actually in use and must have known something about the matter.

NOTE

1. The Scrope v. Grosvenor case can be studied in the two large volumes mentioned in the text; *The Controversy between Sir Richard Scrope and Sir Robert Grosvenor in the Court of Chivalry, A.D.* 1385–1390, by Sir Harris Nicolas, K.H.

2. The Grosvenors have never forgotten the lost arms. Hugh Grosvenor, the first Duke of Westminster, named his famous racehorse the 1880 Derby winner, Bend Or, in memory of the arms. The second Duke's nickname was Bend Or. The Scropes wear a family tie of blue with diagonal gold stripes derived from their arms.

CHAPTER SIX

THE EARLIEST HERALDIC LITERATURE
in Britain and in Europe. English treatises on Heraldry.

THE earliest treatises on the subject of arms are 200 years later than the first appearance of heraldic devices, and 100 years after the early Rolls of Arms. Still these treatises are of great interest as giving the views of men who saw chivalry in flower and to whom the sight of a knight in full armour bearing arms on surcoat, shield, banner or pennon, was something real and not merely a figure in a picture book.

John of Guildford (*circa* 1394) asks the question—Who can grant arms? which he answers—I say that it is a King, Prince, King of Arms or Herald. Another early writer was Nicholas Upton who wrote *De Studio Militari*. This treatise and that of John of Guildford were printed in 1654 by Sir Edward Bysshe, Garter King of Arms, together with the *Aspilogia* of Sir Henry Spelmann, written in the end of the 16th century. The whole was in Latin and no version of Nicholas Upton in English has been published, although a manuscript translation was made by John Blount, an Oxford student, about 1500. Portions of this translation were published in 1931 by Dr. F. P. Barnard of Oxford (Clarendon Press). Nicholas Upton was a Canon of Salisbury Cathedral, and his book is dedicated to Humphrey, Duke of Gloucester, who died in 1446, and the book may therefore be dated about 50 years later than that of John of Guildford. There is a chapter on the assumption of arms which is important, and from which the following quotation is taken.

"We come now to the question lately raised, whether arms bestowed by the favour of princes or of some other lord are better or of such dignity as arms taken by a man's own authority. It has been said above that it has been committed to each noble to take arms and ensigns to himself as he pleased. I have said something on this question in my book on the feudal lord. In understanding this question it must be noted that there are four ways in which we may have arms. (i) We have arms which we bear from our ancestors, a manner well known and frequent. There is no need to dwell on this, because this is known to be the best way. (ii) We have arms by our own merits as most clearly appears by what I have said in my third book in the chapter on the colour red, where I have treated the apposition of the arms of the French King which was made by our supreme lord Henry, now King of England, through that unconquered first borne son (Prince Edward) of Edward III, then King of England, after the capture of the said King of France, John, in the battle at Poitiers. This was indeed rightly added and justly done, as I said there. Thus also could some poor archer who has taken a prince or other distinguished lord, rightly acquire for himself and his heirs the arms of the prisoner thus taken by him, as I have there said. (iii) We have arms which we bear from the favour of a prince or other lords, and note here, that arms which we receive from grant of a prince, are not queried since a prince does not desire this, unless someone shall have borne these arms before. (iv) We have arms which we bear taken by our own authority as we see openly in these days as many poor men who have toiled in the French war have been ennobled, some by prudence, some by force of character, some by courage, some by other qualities. These men, as I have said above, are ennobled, many of whom assume arms of their own authority, to be borne by themselves and their heirs. The names of these there is no need to recount here. I will confess, however, that though arms thus assumed are freely and lawfully borne, they have not as much dignity and authority as those which are granted by the authority of princes and lords. But arms assumed by one's own authority are valid enough, provided they have not been borne by anyone else before. Nor would I dare to approve the opinion of those who say that heralds can grant arms, but I say if arms are borne which are granted by a herald those arms are of no greater authority than arms taken by a man's own authority."

Dr. Barnard in his work already referred to—*The Essential Portions of Nicholas Upton's De Studio Militari*—gives extracts from Blount's MSS. translation, and one of these extracts is entitled "Upton's ruling as to the assumption of arms" which is reproduced above together with its context. Dr. Barnard comments that this chapter of Upton's "puts briefly, but clearly, what was the practice in later mediaeval times, that is in the golden days of chivalry". He also adds in a note: "Indeed this (i.e. the assumption of arms at a man's own pleasure) was the universal view of the lawyers of the 14th and 15th centuries". He goes on to refer to Upton's chapter *De Bove* (page 154 of Bysshe's edition). Upton says, "Therefore to bear in one's arms a bull or bulls, or the heads of bulls, is a sign that at first he who bore those arms was castrated or a eunuch, or so mutilated in his private parts, as through the wars, that he could no longer use his powers. As to give an instance. I once assigned arms—*argent three bulls' heads sable*— to a certain noble knight of the county and family of my lord and master, because he had been quite pierced through his private parts by a lance at the battle of Verneuil. He is, I believe, still living, and bears these arms, and they are good!" Here is a clear case in which a private person was evidently asked to grant arms and did so.

One of the most interesting cases of heraldic writing comes from a lady, for *The Boke of St. Albans* is almost certainly by Dame Juliana Berners of whom very little else is known beyond her authorship of this book. She is supposed to have been Prioress of Sopwell, a nunnery near St. Albans, and in this latter abbey the book was first printed, hence the name usually given to the volume. This book contains a Treatise of Hawking, of Hunting, of Coat Armour, Fishing with an Angle, and Blazing of Arms. The third and fifth portions of the work concern Heraldry, but the whole represents a dissertation on some of the main accomplishments of a 15th century gentleman. The lady needed to have come from a gentle family!

Dame Juliana is supposed to have followed Upton. In her fifth section she certainly incorporated a great deal of his treatise. Nevertheless there is new matter bearing on the subject. "Note here well who shall give coat armours. There shall none of the 9 orders of regality but all only the sovereign king give coat armours. For this is to him impropriated by law of arms. And yet the King shall not make a knight without coat armour before." This would seem to favour the views of those who contend that none but "properly granted" arms are genuine. But alas for the dogmatist! With the delightful inconsistency which marks so many ancient writers Dame

Juliana follows her dictum with another. "Every knight chieftain in the field may make a coat armour knight". Other chapters describe the case of a man whose father had not coat armour, but whose mother had, and he may bear his mother's coat of arms. Again "some men say that a Christian man overcoming a Christian man fighting in the list shall bear the coat armour of him that is overcome." The Dame has no doubt that "a yeoman christened may bear the arms of a gentleman Saracen (i.e. pagan) if he kill him."

So far we have been considering only English writers. Now John of Guildford referred to Bartholus as a great authority. This Bartholus or Bartolo of Sassoferrato was a well-known mediaeval jurist who died about 1356. He has been styled the father of international law (G. C. Cheshire, *Private International Law*, 1949, page 30). He lived from 1314 to 1356 and was professor of law at Bologna, Pisa, and Perugia in turn. His book, *Tractatus de Insigniis et Armis*, is the earliest known treatise on Heraldry. The English writers of these early times follow him closely, quoting him as decisive on disputed points. His treatise can be seen in the British Museum in a copy dated 1475 in crabbed black letter Latin. It takes up 12 pages in this version but can be more easily read in the copy made by Sir Edward Bysshe in his notes of the text of Nicholas Upton, also in E. J. Jones' *Mediaeval Heraldry* (pages 224-52). In the relevant portion of the book Bartholus says, after dealing with the arms proper to princes:

"There are certain insignia or arms of private men or nobles or of peoples, among these are some who bear arms and insignia which have been granted to them by the Emperor or some other lord, as I have seen granted to many by the most serene prince Charles the Fourth (Holy) Roman Emperor and King of Bohemia. To me also, his councillor, he granted arms among the rest, so that I and others of my family should bear a red lion double tailed on a field of gold. That such persons are able to bear arms there can be no doubt. For it is sacrilege to dispute the power of a prince.

"In addition, some take arms to themselves of their own authority and it should be considered whether this is lawful. And I think that this is lawful, just as names were invented to distinguish men. In this way insignia were invented for the same purpose, and just as one is allowed to take names at pleasure, so too one may take arms and place them on his own shield but not on another's.

"But question: if one bears certain arms, or insignia, and another wishes to bear the same arms, is it lawful or can it be forbidden? It appears that he can bear them because anyone can bear another's name."

Bartholus gives careful consideration to the position of persons who, not being of the same blood, yet have the same arms. "For instance a German went to Rome in the time of indulgence where he found a certain Italian who bore the arms of his ancestors. He wished to complain of this. But indeed he could not, for so great is the distance between both places or homes, that the former man could not be injured by this." Bartholus agrees that a skilful smith who puts a mark on his sword and whose workmanship makes his weapons sought after, ought to be able to protect his own trademark; so too should notaries and mapmakers. "What then," he asks, "is the value of a grant of arms from a prince? First, that is of greater dignity. Second, that no one can prohibit one from wearing them. Third, because if two persons assume the same arms, and there appears no difference in priority, he is preferred who had his arms from the prince. Fourth, if one is in the army or in any other place, and questions arise as to precedence, those arms should be preferred which are granted by a prince."

I have let these old writers speak for themselves. They wrote in days when coat armour was in use and they themselves were constantly seeing the living illustration of armory around them. Armory or Heraldry grew up to meet a practical need and was not under a centralised control until a late period. Heralds did not come into existence until after Heraldry had begun—that should seem as obvious as the fact that registrars of births must necessarily be preceded by births. At first heralds were un-official personages who were reckoned among the domestics of a great man's household and who were in the King's household just as in any other. In Scotland to this day there are cases in which the private herald still exists, for instance the Countess of Erroll has the Slains Pursuivant who is her private herald. Scotland is quite a museum of old heraldic things partly due to the fact as we shall see later that in Scotland, Heraldry has been for a long time regulated by the law of the land and so ancient heraldic forms and usages have been preserved.

The functions of the heralds developed because among other things it was useful to have lists of arms and their users. The Rolls of Arms to which I referred in the last chapter were thus compiled not by officials such as we now meet in the College of Arms or in the Lyon Office in Scotland but by men who had an amateur's interest in the subject and who might perhaps have some semi-official appointment with a great man or with the King. The *Armorial de Berry*, the earliest Roll of Arms in Scotland, was made by a French royal herald, Gilles le Bouvier, who was appointed Berry King of Arms and premier herald of France. Despite his official position, or perhaps because of it (for heralds were used as envoys and ambassadors) he travelled widely and recorded the arms of persons in France, England, Scotland, Germany, Italy and other countries. He went to the homes of noblemen or gentlemen whose arms he wished to record and no doubt received their hospitality. This explains some gaps in his work. In some cases the lord of the castle was not at home, in others Gilles le Bouvier did not think it worth while to enter part of the country (that is in Scotland) because he might not be paid for his efforts. A herald did not always enter arms in the Roll unless he were likely to be paid. In his preface to the Roll, le Bouvier adds that he was guided neither by love nor hate in setting down arms, but put them exactly as they were given to him. In other words he exercised no official control but accepted the coats on the guarantee of their bearers; this was a valuable fact in connection with the question of official control of arms during the mediaeval period when the arms bearer was a formidable and frequently fiery warrior, and the herald a pacific officer largely dependent on the hospitality and largesse of his patrons.

A great change was about to be made in the whole position of Heraldry and control in one form or another was to be exercised in different European countries. This will be dealt with in our next chapter.

Those who wish to study the earliest heraldic literature in England at greater length would do well to refer to a treatise by H. Stanford London, entitled "Some Medieval Treatises on English Heraldry". This has been reprinted from *The Anti-*

quaries Journal, i.e. the *Journal of the Society of Antiquaries of London,* Vol. XXXIII, July–October 1953, numbers 3, 4. At the end of the Treatise is an Appendix which lists some 20 mediaeval treatises on English Heraldry.

CHAPTER SEVEN

THE END OF MEDIAEVAL HERALDRY
*with the Wars of the Roses. The growing
control of coats of arms by Kings who set up
Colleges of Arms.*

THE Sovereign of Britain is termed—and has been for many
ages—the Fountain of Honour, dispensing titles and honours according to his or her pleasure. This concept it may be
noted is not universal in Europe. In Poland for instance the
representatives of the great families always contested most
strongly the power of the Crown to create titles. In Poland a
kind of aristocratic anarchy or self government—whichever is
preferred—prevailed. The nobles prided themselves on being
noble *ab initio*, as it were sprung from aristocratic cave men,
and they therefore refused to accept any new nobility created
by the King. New nobles could only come in by adoption and
that gradually through generations. Now in England titles were
at one time to a certain extent not entirely dependent upon the
Sovereign. Instances occur of knighthoods conferred upon
persons by great nobles or churchmen. However, in the usage
of titles the conferring of them soon came to be reserved to the
King's hands or at least was at the most delegated by him.

With arms the position was very different. It is quite clear
that arms originated at the pleasure of the persons concerned.
There are many cases beside those given in previous chapters in
which we find that in a particular area many of the armigerous
families used the charges on the arms of a great family. In
Cheshire the families of knights such as the Grosvenors used
charges from the arms of the old Earls of Chester; so too in
more modern times have many of the Cheshire boroughs.
Arms, unlike titles, were matters of utilitarian purpose and
helpful in warfare. They came gradually to have the quality of
honour which was eventually to disassociate them from the
utilitarian exigencies of warfare and to render talk of shields,
crests and helmets a matter of formality only. Whereas titles
are in their essence matters appertaining to the Crown, the

warlike usages of heraldry were not at first a matter for its recognition; it was only when families began to be proud of their arms and to look down on others who might be using them that the Crown was called in, to decide. Moreover, the Crown made strenuous exertions to gain control of the whole heraldic field. One of the first European instances of this and the first recorded in England is in 1418, when Henry V, about to set out for France, issued a writ to various sheriffs of counties. The translation of this writ from Latin is as follows:

"Whereas, as we are informed, (of) divers men who on our journeys heretofore made, assumed unto themselves arms and coats of arms called coat armour, in cases where neither they nor their ancestors in times gone by used such arms and coats of arms, and proposed to make use of them in our present journey, now, God willing, just about to be made; and although the Almighty distributes his favours in nature according to his will, equally to the rich man and to the poor; nevertheless we, willing that each of our lieges aforesaid should be held and considered as his rank demands charge you to cause to be publically proclaimed on our behalf, in all places within your Bailiwick, whereby our writ we have lately commanded proclamations to be made for the holding of musters, that no one, of whatsoever rank, degree or condition he may be, shall assume such arms or coats of arms, unless he possesses or ought to possess the same in right of his ancestors, or by the gift of some person, having adequate power for that purpose. And that he shall plainly show forth, on the day of his mustering, by whose gift he holds those arms or coats of arms, to the persons for this purpose by us assigned or to be assigned those excepted who bore arms with us at the battle of Agincourt, under pain of not being admitted to take part in the journey aforesaid in the train of him by whom he may have been retained, and of the loss of wages received by him on the said account, together with the stripping off and breaking up of the arms and coats called coat armours aforesaid, on his mustering aforesaid, if they shall have been displayed or found on him. And this you are in no wise to omit. Witness the King at the city of New Sarum, 2 June."

The case of those who claim that the granting of arms rested always and solely with the Crown—and that such is the present position—depends upon this writ of Henry V. The writ is accordingly worth some examination. It will be noticed that arms which have been granted by a sufficient personage, or which are inherited from an ancestor who may have assumed them for himself are not barred. The real purpose of the writ is to prevent the use of self assumed arms in the counties to which the writ was addressed (in the south of England) and in the expedition to France then contemplated. Even so those who had fought upon St. Crispin's day, when Henry and his happy few had struck the French King's crown into the hazard, are purposely excepted and are to be allowed what arms they please. In any event the writ is of limited and local application. Even so it is the only document which specifically lays down a direction from the Crown on the subject of arms. England in the Middle Ages, as later, was prone to imitate many of the polite usages of France. In 1406 Charles VI of France had made the heralds of his household into a close body, giving them a charter of incorporation. Perhaps Henry V was influenced by this action of the French King. Perhaps if there had not been such troubled times in the 15th century, the French example would have been followed earlier in England. However, it was not until 1484 that Richard III incorporated the heralds of his household. They were given a charter with privileges and duties. They were given a building in Coldharbour, London, though on the accession of Henry VII they had to leave it and reside at a monastic establishment near Charing Cross until the reign of Edward VI. They then moved into a building on the site of the College of Arms in Queen Victoria Street, and the present edifice dates from after the Great Fire of London. In the charter of Richard III which incorporated the College, reference is made to John Writh, Garter King of Arms of the English, Thomas Holme, Clarenceux King of Arms, for the southern part of England, John More, Norroy King of Arms for the northern parts, and Richard Champney, Gloucester King of Arms for Wales. Garter, Clarenceux and Norroy are the titles borne by the three Kings of Arms at the College at the present day, as we shall see in the next chapter. William Berry, who was for fifteen years registering clerk to the College of Arms in the early 19th century, and who used a great deal of his officially acquired knowledge in an unofficial manner, says in his *Encyclopedia Heraldica* or *Dictionary of Heraldry*: "That intimate connexion with France, which was occasioned by the claims of the English princes to the Crown of that country, seems to have led to the establishment of heraldic officers, with the names and capacities which they still possess; at least, such establishment is contemporaneous with the invasions of France. Edward III appointed four of the six heralds who form a part of the present constituted body: his successor appointed other officers and these were collected into a college and acted together by order of Henry the Fifth, and by Richard the Third were granted a charter and very extensive privileges."

The growth of the power of the royal heralds was accelerated by the blows dealt to the nobility of the country by the Wars of the Roses. Many nobles were killed, many attainted or deprived of their titles and accordingly the status of the private herald became parlous and very soon it was only in the royal household that heralds flourished. To this day the officers of the College of Arms, thirteen in all, are members of Her Majesty's household and not civil servants, or government appointees. They receive but scanty salaries, these being still the same as in the days of their Tudor establishment. Had their salaries been allowed to keep pace with the changes in the values of money since the 1500s, the Heralds would even so have been woefully underpaid. £20 per year as a salary now is useless, but had it gone up to £200 it would still have been useless. In fact the Heralds from time immemorial have been allowed to charge fees. At first this took the form of actually asking for fees from the newly created knights and lords. "Largesse, largesse, noble knights" the heralds would cry and receive it in a degree suitable to the generosity or ostentation of the giver. To-day and for some centuries the largesse has taken the form of fees for their services, such as granting arms, enrolling pedigrees in their books, checking historical details and many other smaller functions.

Notes on Sources

William Berry, *Encyclopedia Heraldica* or *Dictionary of Heraldry*, edition of 1828.

E

The Rev. Mark Noble, *History of the College of Arms*, written in 1804, and interesting for its style and outlook but as a history superseded by Sir Anthony Wagner's *Heralds of England—A History of the Office and College of Arms*, 1967.

Records and Collections of the College of Arms, by Sir Anthony Wagner. (1951).

Robson, *British Herald*, edition 1830.

The Right to Bear Arms, by X, published by Elliot Stock in 1900. X is usually considered to be A. C. Fox-Davies. All statements within it are to be taken with reserve.

CHAPTER EIGHT

THE HERALDS' VISITATIONS

The control of arms from the 15th century onwards. The Court of Chivalry.

THE head of the College of Arms is the Duke of Norfolk by virtue of his hereditary office of Earl Marshal. This office has been entailed in the family of Howard of which the Duke is the head, ever since 1677. The entailment was made by Act of Parliament after the Marshalship had been held intermittently in the Howard family from 1483. Under the Duke are three kings of Arms—Garter, Clarenceux, and Norroy; six Heralds—Windsor, Chester, Lancaster, Richmond, Somerset and York; four Pursuivants or followers, the lowest of the Heralds, who were originally attendants upon the Heralds as they in their turn were upon the nobility and the Sovereign. The four Pursuivants are Rouge Croix, Blue Mantle, Rouge Dragon and Portcullis. Kings, Heralds and Pursuivants are all loosely included under the general term of Herald at the present time. Most of these picturesque titles are English and derive from geographical sources, unlike the majority of heraldic terms which are French. The Garter office was instituted by Henry V for the service of the Most Noble Order of the Garter and Garter King was on this account given precedence over, and control of, the remaining Heralds. In his patent Garter was called the principal King of English Arms. Clarenceux and Norroy are of older origin than Garter, having been instituted respectively by the Duke of Clarence (whence Clarenceux), third son of Edward III and by Edward II, or at least in his time. The jurisdiction of the Garter King is peculiarly concerned with the arms of peers and baronets, and he is also in fact the secretary of the Earl Marshal and as such it is his business to deal with all manner of problems. The tasks to which Garter may be called are manifold, and may include the question whether arms can be granted for instance to a corporate institution which is engaged in profit making. The jurisdiction of the other two Kings is provincial, Clarenceux having control of matters armorial in the south, east and west parts of England, while Norroy (i.e. North Roi or King) controls the northern parts of England, above the river Trent.

Of the six Heralds all except Windsor, "who has his denomination from the royal castle or palace, take their titles from counties and shires which have been at sundry times the honours or appendages of younger sons of the crown" (Robson, in his *British Herald*, page 34). Windsor Herald was created by Edward III when he was in France. Edward had been born at Windsor, was known as Edward of Windsor and was very fond of his birthplace. He greatly enlarged the castle there and it was at Windsor that the festivities in connection with the institution of the Order of the Garter were held, just as they were in 1948 on the sixth centenary of the Order's foundation. It was therefore very natural for the King to name his new Herald after Windsor.

Lancaster Herald is mentioned as early as 1347, and was probably connected with the title of the King's fourth son, John of Gaunt, Duke of Lancaster. Chester is also said to have been instituted by Edward, but the office of this Herald can be traced with certainty only from the reign of Richard II. Edward III was himself Earl of Chester when he was Prince of Wales, and the title is usually borne by the sovereign's eldest son. Yet another heraldic creation ascribed to Edward III is that of York Herald in honour of his fifth son Edmund of Langley, Duke of York. So much heraldic activity on the part of Edward III need not cause surprise. In his reign the eyes of Christendom were fixed upon the English Sovereign and his people. English soldiers proved their courage and success in France, Scotland, Spain and the Low Countries, and on the sea. Great victories favoured the banners of Edward and the Black Prince, and the fantastic chivalry of the Middle Ages reached its height, thereafter to decline steeply into the treacheries, cruelties and bestialities of the 15th century.

The institution of Somerset Herald is ascribed to Henry VIII, in honour of his natural son, Henry Fitzroy, Duke of Richmond and Somerset; the office of Richmond Herald occurs in the reign of Edward IV. Various other titles have been borne by English heralds from time to time and from different circumstances connected with our kings, e.g. Guienne King of

Arms, an office held by Sir Payne Roelt, a native of Hainault, whose daughter Katharine Swinford (the name of her first husband) became the mistress and eventual wife of John of Gaunt, the "time-honoured Lancaster" of Shakespeare and the mother of several children from one of whom descended the

College of Arms.

Tudor dynasty. This office of Guienne bore relation to the extensive territories in the south-west of France held by the English Crown for 300 years from the time of Henry II to that of Richard II (the latter was always known as Richard of Bordeaux). On the capture of these territories by the French the *raison d'etre* of the office of Guienne King ceased.

Of the four Pursuivants, Rouge Croix may derive his title

from the red cross of St. George. He was instituted by Henry V. The latter and Edward III have both been credited with the creation of Blue Mantle, the origin of the name coming from the description of the royal arms of France, *azure semeé de lis* (i.e. sprinkled with lilies). Edward III assumed the arms of France in right of his mother—the she-wolf of France, as Gray called her—as heiress to the French throne. He placed them in the first and fourth quarters of his shield, having precedence over England, and this position was maintained for 460 years until the reign of George III (1800). Rouge Dragon and Portcullis were created by Henry VII, the latter being named after the portcullis badge used by Henry. Rouge Dragon is an allusion to the dragon device of the Welsh princes from whom the new King derived his lineage.

The charter of King Richard III which incorporated the College in 1484 assigned for the use of the Heralds a building called Cold Harbour, formerly called Poultney's Inn, in the parish of All Saints the Little in the City of London. When Richard fell at Bosworth, the Heralds lost their chief, the Duke of Norfolk being killed also. The grant of Cold Harbour was declared void, and it was not until the Heralds obtained a new charter from Edward VI reaffirming their privileges, and that Mary I looked with favour upon them, that they were granted a property called Derby House "situated in the parish of St. Benedict and St. Peter within the city of London, to be held by them in free burgage of the City of London". Derby House was totally destroyed in the Great Fire of London, 1666, and until the College was rebuilt, the Heralds had temporary rooms in Whitehall and later in the palace of Westminster. The new College was finished in 1683 and Robson, writing in 1830 describes it as consisting of an extensive range of quadrangular buildings, "one of the handsomest and best edifices in London" (*op. cit.* p. 36). Thus the College has continued for more than two and a half centuries to occupy a site which has come to be dominated more and more by the buildings of modern commerce and where the College with the ancient city churches forms one of the few relics of the old City of London.

It was from this strengthened and revived College of Arms that the Heralds went out to hold the Heralds' Visitations in the 16th and 17th centuries. What exactly were these Visita-

tions? They were a new departure in the recording of arms, for
they combined almost from the start the recording of pedigrees
with that of arms, and thus the Heralds acquired a genealogical
function which they have never lost. The Visitations were a
continuation of the old Rolls of Arms and a new form of
recording matters armorial, but they were also part of the
Tudor scheme of government. The Tudors had a centralised
monarchy and it was natural for them to try to bring the
control of arms completely under the royal sway. The Visitations began in the reign of Henry VIII when in 1530 the royal
commission was first given under the great seal authorising the
officers of arms to visit particular counties of England, to
register arms and pedigrees of the nobility and gentry of those
parts, and to reprove and control those who laid claim to arms
which they had no right to use according to the rules of arms.

The Visitations were tours of inspection undertaken by the
Heralds throughout England at various periods between 1530
and 1688, for after the abdication of James II no further
commissions were issued to hold them. There is thus a period of
160 years during which the counties of England were covered
by the Heralds. The records of their researches remain, and
many have been printed, notably in the series of publications of
the Harleian Society. There was no apparent system in these
Visitations. Kent was visited in 1552, 1558, 1570, 1612, 1634
and 1664-8. Contrast this record of a home county with that of
Westmorland, visited in 1530 and not again until 1615.
Durham had four Visitations, in each case by Norroy King of
Arms, in 1530, 1575, 1615, and 1666. Cumberland and
Cornwall alike received but three, with wide intervals between
the second and third. The journeys to the more distant parts of
the country were rendered difficult by the bad state of the roads
and by perils from highwaymen.

Once arrived in a county, it was the habit of the visiting
Herald to take up his abode with the principal gentleman of the
neighbourhood. His presence was proclaimed and the local
gentry were required or requested to come in for registration.
The task took a long time to carry out properly and was often
skimped. Then the actual registration presented difficulties. All
had to be done by hand, and in recording the pedigrees the
heralds experienced the same problems as a modern editor

when he asks for exact dates of birth, marriage and death. Few people can give these dates for their parents without consulting documents or other persons, and consequently few of the pedigrees recorded in the first Visitations go back beyond the great-grandfather of the man giving the information. The first Visitation of Kent in 1530-1, a slim volume of 22 pages gives hardly any dates in its pedigrees. (*Harleian Society publn.* Vol. LXXIV). They seldom extend beyond three generations, and are often limited to a statement of paternity alone. The genealogical function was new to the Heralds but they undertook it with growing skill. The primary çoncern was with arms but genealogy enters into Heraldry and vice-versa.

In the course of the Visitations it became in some counties the practice for the Heralds to combine the record of various inspections in the same manuscript. The 1530 Visitation of Sussex is continued and enlarged by the combination of the Visitation of the same county in 1633. This practice implies a continuity in the work and shows how its genealogical aspect was becoming more prominent. In most of the MSS. the arms ascribed to the family are tricked or drawn at the head of the pedigree. The illustrations are usually in black and white and show the quarterings of the family's marriage alliances. Very little is known by the majority of people who are interested in Heraldry about the Visitations even when their own families have figured in them, so that some details about the conduct of the Visitations will be interesting.

In some of the early Visitation records the narrative form of pedigree is used, but this soon gives place to the tabular style with which most people are familiar from the genealogical tables of the Kings of England in their history books. (For the necessary connection between Heraldry and Genealogy see the last two chapters of this book). In the Visitations of Berkshire (*Harleian Soc.* Vol. LVI, 1907), that of 1623 contains tabular pedigrees, but the earlier Visitations of 1532 and 1566 give the pedigrees in narrative form. As one glances through the records of the Visitations it is possible to see the growth in the number of families who applied for arms or had a confirmation of arms where some doubt had arisen. (There is even now a technical difference between a grant and a confirmation, but the man who nowadays obtains a confirmation from the College of Arms will find that he has to pay the same fees as for a grant!) In the days of slow travelling and difficult communications many families would never have visited London to apply for a grant, and the arrival of the Heralds in their neighbourhood must have been a boon. Nevertheless the majority of the arms recorded are registered simply as borne and as not infringing the rights of any other person. The fact that grants are quoted where they occur proves that in most other cases no grant existed, but the arms were simply in use and were then recorded by the Heralds. In the commissions to the Officers of Arms powers were granted to them to deface and mutilate monuments which bore arms used without authority, to proclaim publicly that persons to whom the Heralds confirmed no authority to bear arms were not entitled to them and to require disclaimers of the use of arms from such persons. But the use of these powers does not seem to have been extensive, and we may note the sympathetic attitude taken by the Heralds to arms which were in use. In the Visitation of Rutland 1681-82 a list of disclaimers is given. These persons have agreed that "not being able to show any good proof or right to either of those titles (Esquire or Gentleman), nor knowing at present of any arms belonging to us, do hereby disclaim all such attributes and arms and do promise henceforth to forbear to make use of either, until such times as we can by lawful authority do the same." A clue as to the reasons for the disclaimers may be found by looking through the list of them and seeing the notes attached by the visiting officers. George Austin was described by the bailiff who had made the return of the gentlemen of the neighbourhood "to be a good farmer but no pretender to arms." A schoolmaster and an attorney are not allowed, likewise a draper and a wealthy yeoman who had £100 a year. Richard Cheseldyne who was a captain in the trained bands (or territorials as we might say) renounced arms, but the Herald adds, "Yet I am informed he uses the arms of Cheseldyne."

The old problems of social position obviously affected the Heralds' decisions. Persons who lived in the style expected of an English gentleman were allowed arms, others were not, and there were borderline cases. We are used to the 18th century description of an attorney as rascally, and perhaps the Heralds who visited Rutland may have felt the same. There seems little doubt that lawyers, both sides of the profession, elbowed their way into the cohorts of gentility about 200 years ago, and are now firmly entrenched as esquires. As to doctors there is still a considerable doubt, according to official heraldic views, as to whether they can be classed as gentlemen.

Turning from the disclaimers in this Visitation of Rutland we see how reasonable the Heralds were in dealing with persons who had some claim to gentility. The Busbys of Barlithorpe used arms which had been described and entered in the Visitation in 1618. They are tricked again in the Visitation of 1681 with a note to the effect that they were so very near those of Sir John Busby of Addington in Buckinghamshire that there was hardly "a sufficient difference between them, especially no relation appearing between the families." In the case of the Matthews of Oakham only a red wax seal was produced by the family in proof of the arms and the herald was unable to find justification for their use. Nevertheless they were entered with the Matthews' pedigree and there is no note that they were "respited for proof". When this latter entry appears in a Visitation it means that a period of six months was allowed for the family to find proof of their right to arms. When no proof was forthcoming, the arms were reckoned not to be of authority. In some cases owing to the cessation of the Visitations after 1688, families have continued in a state of suspended animation as regards their arms. A notable case of respite for proof not being followed up is that of the Lloyds of Brewood, where nothing has been done for over two and a half centuries, a lengthy continuation of the six months allowed.

In the case of Beauchamp of Branston the head of the family was able to produce only a signet and tablet of his arms, and although these were tricked with the pedigree, there is a note that "they do not seem to be above 30 years standing and therefore not allowable." At this time (16th and 17th century) the Heralds were accustomed to accept arms although not granted by them, if they had been borne for a sufficient period and if the users were persons of gentility. This is what is known as the right to arms by prescription and user, a right which undoubtedly did exist in England in the not remote past but the mere mention of which now makes some heraldic pundits seethe with rage. As to the period that obviously had to be more than 30 years. One of the present Kings of Arms of the College of Arms, Sir Anthony Wagner, in his *Heralds and Heraldry in the Middle Ages*, quotes from MSS. of the College of Arms that arms claimed by families must have been borne and used by them for 60 years at least before the claim was made. He also quotes what is considered to be an instruction for a Visitation issued by Sir William Dugdale between 1683 and 1686, in which arms borne by prescription are to be allowed if it can be demonstrated that the lineal ancestors of the claimant have made use of them above 80 years past at the least (*op. cit.*, pp. 2-3).

This is a fair summing up of the heraldic practice in allowing arms which the claimant's ancestors had, in effect, assumed themselves. Consequently it is extraordinary to read in some modern heraldic books, statements that no such thing as a right to prescription exists. Perhaps the explanation is that most heraldic books nowadays are written by people who have no claim to prescription or ancient arms, and as they or their immediate forbears have purchased arms to themselves at a great price they cannot bear the thought that someone else may have arms without paying for them.

The period of prescription varied according to the strictness of the particular Herald, but it was evidently never less than 60 years or two generations. The most interesting point about this recognition of arms borne by prescription is that the period runs for 60 or 80 years before the time of making the claim. It might have been thought that the time should have run for 60 years before the foundation of the College in 1484, or before the commencement of the Visitations in 1530. At either of these dates the vast majority of English arms were borne by prescription, being self granted. There are instances of arms being granted by the Heralds before the foundation of the College, but they are not numerous, and no famous coat of the Middle Ages—Percy, Courtenay, Talbot—springs from this source. By 1530 more grants had occurred, but even so the position of the majority of arms would not have been affected. Consequently at the beginning of the Visitations, the Heralds would have been compelled to accept the bulk of arms as being borne by prescription. After 150 years of the Visitations, however, it would have been reasonable to say that claims to arms by user could only be allowed if they went back before 1530. Instead, the Heralds were willing to allow arms by prescription provided they had been borne for two generations at least before the claim was made—and the claim could be made at any time. In other words, the right of adopting arms which had existed from the earliest days of armory is here recognised subject only to confirmation by the Heralds. That this should come from Sir William Dugdale towards the end of his life is the more remarkable because of the immense reputation which he had as an antiquary. In his own work we encounter examples of the working of the heraldic law. In the Visitation of Derbyshire (1662, reviewed 1663, printed by Golding and Lawrence, London, 1879) there are the arms of Morewood entered with the note "no proof", and another note that an altered coat had been granted to the family in 1678. The arms of Akney are allowed with the note that they are really the proper coat of Inwardby, whose daughter and co-heiress married Abney or Akney; a hard text for those who argue that arms cannot be adopted by a man on marriage with an heiress. In some half a dozen cases the arms are described as not proved, but the majority are accepted and difference marks duly noted where cadet lines are found. (A cadet is a younger member of a family, in practice the term includes anyone except the head of the family and his wife. Difference marks are marks placed upon a coat of arms to show that the person using the arms is not the head of the family.)

In Sir William Dugdale's *Visitation of Yorkshire* 1665-1666 (*Surtees Society*, Vol. XXXVI, 1859) we have a valuable indication as to the thoroughness of the heraldic inspections, and as to the members of families who were not at home when the Heralds called. Nearly one-third of the gentry required by Dugdale to produce proof of arms and pedigree failed even to respond. Two years after the Visitation, Dugdale issued a list of these persons, with a warning that they were not to use the arms and titles on pain of penalties from the Earl Marshal. As the editor of the Visitations justly remarked, the descendants of many of these families would have rejoiced had they then placed their pedigrees upon record. In the case of Foljambe of Steveton, Dugdale stated that "this family have for many ages used their arms with supporters" and he records the supporters.

Taylor of Templehurst referred Dugdale to the Visitation of Shropshire "but there is nothing there". Simpson of Wetherby has respite given "for exhibiting the arms but nothing done". There is so much in these entries which is reminiscent of the difficulties of an editor of *Burke's Peerage* or *Landed Gentry* to-day in seeking for information that one can have every sympathy with the difficulties of the Heralds.

Cadency Marks.

After the flight of James II in 1688 no further commissions were issued by the Sovereign to the Officers of Arms to enable them to hold Visitations. These inspections of the Heralds had never been popular with the gentry of England because they were a restriction on their freedom and as we can see even after the Visitations had been going on for 100 to 150 years there were still many families using arms which had not been registered, or granted. Many families did not bother to attend the Visitations, or if they did, persisted in using arms which had been denied to them by the visitors. The monarchs who succeeded James II owed their thrones to the gentry who dominated Parliament and did not feel secure enough to issue commissions to their Heralds to inspect and interfere with the arms of the ancient gentry of the realm.

Apart however from the Visitations there was another form of arms control which was in use in the Tudor and Stuart period and that was by means of the Court of Chivalry. This was an ancient institution which gradually lost the bulk of its jurisdiction and therefore became somewhat of an anachronism. It never disappeared, but remained in a state of suspended animation for 200 years to be revived in our own time. It is so important in the history of Heraldry that it should have a chapter to itself.

CHAPTER NINE

THE COURT OF CHIVALRY

its abolition and its restoration after the restoration of the monarchy in 1660, discontinuance in 1735 and revival in 1954-55.

IN December 1954 there occurred in England an event of heraldic importance which it is improbable could have taken place in any other country in the world. This was the revival of the Court of Chivalry which had not sat for 219 years. The circumstances were as follows:

The nature of the Court of Chivalry has been much misunderstood. Its name has been given as that of a Court Military or Court Martial and from this it was assumed that the Court of Chivalry was the origin of the courts martial known to everyone connected with the armed forces. This is not correct and is based on a wrong translation of the Latin name of the court, *Curia Militaris* (where Miles means knight) and so the correct translation is Court of Knighthood, i.e. Court of Chivalry. The Court was that of the two great Officers of State, the High Constable and the Earl Marshal. The Court did exercise disciplinary powers in the army. References to a Constable and Marshal are usually found in connection with a mediaeval army, but they by no means indicate on all occasions the presence of the two great functionaries just mentioned. In any event, in the case of war waged simultaneously with France and Scotland, clearly the two could not both be present in the two armies. There were Statutes and Ordinances of War, from which developed the Articles of War, which were eventually embodied in the Mutiny Act of 1689, and so on into the various Army Acts which governed the British Army in recent times. The type of case brought before the Court of Chivalry varied; some were of a kind which later came within the jurisdiction of the Common Law Courts; all were more or less concerned with matters of honour, about the wrongful use of arms, or of opprobrious words, such as a statement that a man was not a gentleman. The office of Lord High Constable was hereditary in the great family of Bohun, but after the extinction of that family the office was held by various persons until 1521 when the last High Constable was Edward Stafford, Duke of Buckingham. The office of Earl Marshal eventually became as we have seen, hereditary in the family of the Duke of Norfolk.

Thomas Wolsey, Cardinal, Archbishop of York.

It is clear that the Court of Chivalry presided over by two great Crown officers, could become an instrument of royal tyranny. In fact, cases of treason were brought before the Court and dealt with in a very summary and often unjust manner. To prevent such abuses, the English Parliament, as early as 1389 passed Statutes to confine the jurisdiction of the Court to "cognizance of contracts touching deeds of arms or of war out of the realm and also things which touch war within the realm which cannot be determined or discussed by the common law."

The Court of Chivalry became very unpopular, and in 1521

the virtual abolition of the office of High Constable struck a blow at its jurisdiction. In that year Cardinal Wolsey, the powerful minister of Henry VIII, brought about the trial, condemnation and execution of the High Constable, the Duke of Buckingham. Wolsey was of humble origin, the son of a butcher in the town of Ipswich. He hated Buckingham and caused his ruin. When the Emperor Charles V heard of this event he exclaimed: "A butcher's cur has pulled down the finest buck in England." After 1521 no High Constable was appointed, except on the day of a Coronation. Thus at the Coronation of Her Majesty Queen Elizabeth II, the famous soldier, Viscount Alanbrooke, was Constable *pro hac vice*, for that day alone.

The disappearance of the High Constable from the Court of Chivalry weakened the position of the Earl Marshal, the remaining functionary. From 1521 however, until the outbreak of the Great Civil War in 1642, the Court continued to sit, but objections were continually made against its jurisdiction. Moreover much of its jurisdiction was lost. Under James I (1603-1625) the right to hear cases of claims to peerages was taken from the Court and given to the House of Lords. With the growth of a regular army from 1645, the military jurisdiction passed away. Under the government of the Parliament and of Oliver Cromwell, the Court of Chivalry was abolished. After the Restoration of Charles II in 1660 the Court was restored. It continued to sit at intervals until 1735, but the cases brought before it were not serious and as many of the defendants in these cases objected to its jurisdiction, it ceased to function. It still existed and perhaps the best testimony to this is that Blackstone the great English legal commentator stated in his 18th century *Commentaries upon the Laws of England* that the Court existed and had jurisdiction in matters armorial. But no one in recent years expected the Court to be revived. From 1718 to 1744 the Garter King of Arms was John Anstis who was succeeded by his son. Great efforts were made by both of them to maintain the Court and then to revive it and the Visitations but nothing came of these efforts. Anstis the elder had wished to use the Court as a means of controlling persons who used arms without the authority of the College. Especially as the Visitations had broken down it was essential to keep up the Court if there were to be any control over arms by the College. It looked, however, after an interval of more than 200 years that the Court was in a state of permanently suspended animation. In 1951 in my book—*The Story of Heraldry*—I wrote: "The Court is in abeyance but not abolished. It could in theory be revived but if the rich English gentry of the 17th and 18th centuries who had limited an ancient monarchy did not care for the continuance of its jurisdiction, is it likely that it can be revived under Socialist influence?" So it appeared, and the failure of the Court to sit was serious. The two methods used by the English heralds to control arms, the Visitations and the Court being gone, there existed no means of controlling arms for 219 years in England and Wales. Heraldic licence prevailed. The position was quite different in Scotland where the use of arms was regulated by law. (See chapter 12). The ordinary Courts of law took no cognizance of arms except in what is known as "names and arms clauses", that is clauses in a will whereby the testator willed that the beneficiary should take the name and arms of the testator as one of the conditions of inheriting his estate. The Probate Court or as it is now the Probate Division of the High Court then dealt with the matter and required the person to comply with the testator's desire as a matter of interpreting and carrying out the testator's will. The change of names and arms had to be registered with the College of Arms because the Court had to have official proof of the change. There was also a tax on the use of arms, but this was purely a financial matter and was levied on arms whether registered at the College or borne of a man's own free will. This tax was abolished in 1945.

For over 200 years the curious position existed that a man could do exactly as he liked in matters armorial in England and Wales whereas in Scotland he was regulated by a strict heraldic law; there was no existing legal compulsion on a person to seek the confirmation of the College of Arms on arms which he had assumed for himself. The realisation of this fact (for no amount of verbal haziness could prevent it being a fact) indicated that the practice of the College of Arms would suffer drastic reductions. It was not long before a move was made to revive the Court of Chivalry, and during the year 1954 this was increasingly rumoured until it became a fact in December

1954. Accordingly on 21 December in that year in the Lord
Chief Justice's Court at the Royal Courts of Justice in the
Strand a test case came before the revived Court. *The Mayor,
Aldermen and Citizens of the City of Manchester* v. *the
Manchester Palace of Varieties Ltd.* There were present the
Earl Marshal in full levée dress, the Surrogate for the Earl
Marshal, that is the Lord Chief Justice, Lord Goddard, who
wore the robes of a Doctor of Civil Law, and six of the
Officers of Arms. These latter, who were also in levée dress and
had their swords at their sides, were the York, Chester,
Lancaster and Somerset Heralds, and the Rouge Dragon and
Blue-mantle Pursuivants. The joint registrars of the Court who
wore academic dress were Mr. Wilfred Maurice Phillips and
Anthony Richard Wagner, the latter being Richmond Herald.
There was a great concourse to hear the Court and admission
was by ticket only. This was natural because after all the
revival of the Court which had 600 years before heard the case
of *Grosvenor* v. *Scrope* did not occur every year. The cause of
the dispute was in one respect ludicrous and in another very
serious. The Manchester Corporation alleged that the defendants, a music hall, had for many years used the Manchester
Corporation arms, duly granted by Queen Victoria, on the drop
curtain of their theatre and also on their company seal. As Lord
Goddard observed in the judgment the former charge would
hardly have justified the case, but the second was a very serious
matter. The use of the Manchester Corporation arms on the
seal of the Manchester Palace of Varieties implied that the
Corporation was in some way responsible for the acts of the
defendants. In the result the judgment (which was read on 21
January 1955) was given against the defendants. Lord
Goddard ruled that the Manchester Palace of Varieties had no
right to use the arms of Manchester City. He prohibited the
Palace of Varieties from using the arms in question and ordered
them to pay the costs of the action, which were agreed at £300.
Thus the jurisdiction of the Court of Chivalry has been upheld
after the extraordinary lapse of 219 years, and it has been
proved that the use of arms can be controlled by the Court. Or
has it? The judgment of the Surrogate, Lord Goddard, is that
of one of the greatest of modern judges and deserves to be read
in all its detail. An analysis of it will be of interest and use.

Nothing short of an Act of Parliament could abolish the Court however long it slumbered. Why then despite its antiquity and its undoubted authority did it fall into disuse? The answer is that the means to enforce its decisions were a matter of great doubt and obscurity. The Surrogate gave a disquisition on the use of coats of arms as a matter of display. He detailed the various forms which the display of arms may take to-day in decoration or embellishment on ensigns, on articles of use such as tobacco jars, ashtrays, pieces of china, and many other articles of which thousands are sold every year by manufacturers who are showing the arms of families or corporations or societies other than their own. He supposed that in strictness none of these uses of coats of arms were permissible, but added that he was by no means satisfied that at the present time it would be right for the Court of Chivalry to be put in motion merely because arms, whether of a corporation or of a family had been displayed in the way of decoration or embellishment. On the other hand he regarded the use by the defendants in the present case of the arms of the City of Manchester on the common seal of the company as being a serious matter, since a deed sealed with an armorial device would thereby be authenticated as the act and deed of the person entitled to bear the arms. Accordingly a clear distinction was drawn between the use of the former kind and the case of display as shown by the use of the Manchester City arms on the pelmet of the company's curtain. To resolve the difficulty and to decide between cases in which a serious infringement of armorial rights has been incurred and those in which a mere harmless display has taken place, the Surrogate made two recommendations:—(1) that the Court should not be set in motion unless leave had been obtained before proceedings were instituted, and that if the Court were to sit again it should be convened only where some really substantial reason for the exercise of its jurisdiction existed. (2) If there were to be any considerable desire to institute proceedings and to use the Court frequently, then the Court should be placed upon a proper statutory basis with a definition of its jurisdiction and the sanctions which it could impose.

To this I would add that unfortunately there would appear to be a difficulty in obtaining the necessary statutory backing.

No institution can survive or continue to function effectively, if it is out of touch with the spirit of the age. Lord Goddard in his judgment mentioned the powers of the old spiritual courts, some of which still exist, but, as he said, it would be unthinkable that a suit involving a criminal cause could now be promoted in the spiritual courts. The reason for this is that ecclesiastical lawyers of the highest eminence consider the jurisdiction of the spiritual courts over the laity to be no longer in accordance with modern thought. Even with the vindication of the Court of Chivalry's jurisdiction established by the recent decision, which distinguishes its practical significance from that of the ecclesiastical courts as they affect laymen, the position of the Court of Chivalry differs considerably from that of the Lord Lyon in Scotland. (See chapter 12). The Court of the latter is part of the judicial system of Scotland with the authority of 300 years of law behind it. It is hard to think that in modern England legislation to reconstitute an ancient court dealing with an archaic subject would find favour in government circles to-day. One can imagine the objections which would be raised by the Socialist party to a Parliamentary Bill which purported to give power to a court concerned solely with matters of dignity and with semi-feudal privileges. The Conservatives would feel awkward about introducing such legislation because of the handle which it would give to their opponents.

Lord Goddard drew attention to the difficulties that would be associated with restraining what may be called the tobacco-jar user of arms. He quoted Bacon's Essay on Judicature: "Penal laws if they have been sleepers of long time or if they have grown unfit for present use should be by wise judges confined in execution" and he suggested that the line should be drawn by the exercise of common sense, and that the functioning of the Court of Chivalry should accordingly depend on leave being obtained before its machinery were set in motion.

The practical upshot of the revival of the Court of Chivalry is to demonstrate the practical difficulty of using the Court. It needs statutory basis for its operations and that statutory basis is most unlikely to be obtained. It is therefore hard to see how people can be prevented from (i) using the arms of other people to whom they are not related or (ii) devising arms for themselves. It is possible that the matter could be remedied by reviving the old system of the Visitations, but here again it may be easily felt by those responsible that they would be running counter to the spirit of the age.

In fact there is nothing to prevent anyone from using what arms he pleases, any more than there has been for the past 200 years. A recognition by the Heralds of the right to prescriptive arms as their predecessors did would make all the difference and be far more effective than any Courts or Visitations to make people willing to take their arms for confirmation to Heralds' College. Also the little detail that charges for recording or confirming arms borne of prescription should be on more reasonable scales than those at present charged.

Reading matter: There is a verbatim report of the case described above in *The High Court of Chivalry* published by the Heraldry Society 1955. Also of use is: *The High Court of Chivalry: A Study of the Civil Law in England* by G. D. Squibb.

CHAPTER TEN

TUDOR HERALDRY

*and the use of Coats of Arms without armour
in decoration in a more extensive manner than
during the Middle Ages.*

H ERALDRY is not only a science but also an art and it is partly due to this fact that it has survived from the Middle Ages when the use of body armour to which it owed its origin began to give way. The other factor in keeping Heraldry alive has been, to put it quite plainly, snobbery. Because only the richest and most powerful persons used arms it soon became the mark of the "best people" and so arms acquired a significance far beyond their merely utilitarian use in war as ensigns. But the heraldic art is a more pleasant subject and we can leave for later chapters a consideration of what is meant by heraldic snobbery.

Bodiam.

Bodiam Castle.
Wardedieux.

Dalyngrigge.

The beauty of the forms and colours used in Heraldry attracts many who have no knowledge of the subject and even some who profess to despise it. Very early use of the shields, crests and other heraldic objects departed from the martial forms which gave rise to Heraldry, and were adapted to peaceful uses. Over the gateway of Bodiam Castle in Sussex, near Hastings, can be seen cut in the stonework the arms of the old Lords of Bodiam, of the Wardedieux, and of the Dalyngrigges. The last named family came into possession of the castle through marriage with the heiress of the second family named, or rather Sir Richard Dalyngrigge who married the heiress of Wardedieux acquired the manor and land of Bodiam, and then obtained from the King, Richard II, the necessary permission to build a castle there. In the museum nearby there can be seen another charming use of Heraldry. The lord and lady of Bodiam are shown, he with his surcoat bearing his

Arms of Clare in stained glass in Salisbury Cathedral, showing lead joints, *c.* 1280.

arms, she with her long gown marked down the middle by a dividing line having on the right hand side the arms of her husband and on the left those of her father's family. This was in fact an example of the impalement method of displaying arms to which reference has already been made. The beautiful result on the long flowing rich gowns of the mediaeval ladies can be imagined, and may be seen in many an illuminated manuscript from the Middle Ages. One wonders that no Hartnell or Fath, with so many aristocratic clients, has tried to revive this beautiful fashion. In this way the use of the coats of arms spread from the battlefield and the tourney to the ladies' bower, and the halls of peace. But to return to the use of the arms over the gateway of Bodiam. By means of this usage it was possible for those conversant with Heraldry to know not only who was the present owner of a mansion but also those who had held it before him. The arms were used on every occasion when the identity of the owner was to be established. The arms were naturally used in connection with the deceased. In the church at Boxgrove near Chichester in Sussex can be seen numerous instances, beautifully restored in this case, of arms of mediaeval persons who had chantries there. In

Arms of Warwick the King Maker, 1470. Window in the Hall of John Halle, Salisbury, showing quarterings of Beauchamp, Neville, Montagu, Newburgh, Clare, Monthermer, and Despenser.

Chichester Cathedral itself there are of course many other examples. It would be hard to find a church or cathedral any portion of which goes back before 1800 where no arms appear. At Speldhurst in Kent, the burial place of the great Waller family, the building is fairly new, as English churches go, because the old church was destroyed over 100 years ago by fire. But there is a collective memorial there to the Wallers with their arms, showing the shield in miniature hanging from the walnut tree crest, this shield being decorated with fleur-de-lis in allusion, it is said, to the capture of the Duke of Orleans at Agincourt by a member of the family. In Worcester Cathedral the arms of bishops are so numerous that they have almost overpowered those of laymen. In Bath Abbey there are few memorials, if any, before 1500, but of the numerous monuments since that date the majority are with coats of arms. The church of St. Peter Port in Guernsey has many coats of arms of local families of importance. In the church at the end of Princes

The earliest English brass: Sir John D'Abernon, 1277, Stoke D'Abernon, Surrey.

Street, Edinburgh (that of St. John, Episcopalian), there are numerous decorative shields; while St. Giles itself is a Westminster Abbey of the north for those who wish to study Heraldry. Indeed the examples which I have given are only a very tiny fraction of those available and available without trouble for the inquirer. There can be very few places in the British Isles were there are no examples of coats of arms used in connection with tombs or memorials of the dead. Among other instances of this particular usage can be cited the brasses on the floors of many churches. The habit of making a brass and putting it on to a tomb no longer obtains, and therefore the number of examples is bound to decrease with the passage of time, but to-day public opinion would not allow anyone to destroy a brass. Many brasses are covered over with a carpet or rug to protect them from damage from the atmosphere or from being trodden upon. This is the case at Stoke D'Abernon, where the brass of Sir John D'Abernon is protected by a rug. The brass was laid over the tomb and on it were shown the knight and usually his lady, his coat of arms being shown on the armour. Fine examples are found in different parts of England. But while this particular use of arms in funerary memorials has ceased, there is no sign that the use of arms over tombs or in memorials will go. It still persists and this in the case of monuments erected for societies and institutions.

Another use of the arms of the deceased was in connection with what were called hatchments. These were wooden boards which were decorated with the arms of the deceased and then put up outside his or her house for some time during the funeral and mourning period. These objects are not quite so out of date as many suppose. In a collection of 1,500 hatchments which the Bath Heraldic Society were able to list, no less than 250 belonged to the last 100 years, and 25 to the present century. Even in the last few years hatchments have still been displayed, e.g. at Oxford on the death of the head of a College, and at Ashburnham House, Sussex, where the arms of the family were shown over the main door of the empty house after the death of the last of the family (Lady Catherine Ashburnham). The Bath Heraldic Society had some years back a record of over 2,000 hatchments in England over the past $3\frac{1}{2}$ centuries. At Chesham Church in Buckinghamshire there are many hatchments preserved in the vestry, and most of these must be at least 200 years old. In some cases the hatchment was deposited over the tomb, hence its survival in churches, in others the hatchment remained the family property and was brought out during the time of mourning. Perhaps hatchments developed from the days when it was customary to put the weapons and shield of the dead knight above his tomb. In

Canterbury Cathedral the arms of the Black Prince were long displayed (now a replica is shown while the original is preserved elsewhere) and on the shield are shown the arms of France quartering England (an allusion to the claim of Edward III to be King of France as well as of England).

Tombs, brasses, hatchments—these were the mouldering honours of the dead, but also the coats of arms of living men were illustrated. In modern days we have the Chequers

Shield of FitzAlan, Earl of Arundel, on the tomb of Edmund of Langley, Duke of York, K.G., fifth son of Edward III—1393, King's Langley, Herts.

window, at the official residence of the Prime Minister, which was redesigned to show the Garter bestowed upon Winston Churchill. Again triumphal emblems are often made of coats of arms. When the new Chamber of the House of Lords was being prepared the question arose of the great window to replace that lost in the air raids of the second world war. So 160 coats of arms of peers renowned in the country's history were selected and these were illustrated in the stained glass.

The use of arms on the gowns of ladies showed the way however to a more peaceful and less death pre-occupied usage of Heraldry. Heraldic emblems came to signify ownership. Just as the retainers of the mediaeval lords wore their lords' badges on their jerkins, so in more modern times the footmen and menservants wore livery, the latter being in the principal colours of the arms of the employer and the arms themselves or the badge were often shown on the buttons of the servant.

Shield of Sir Winston Spencer Churchill, K.G.
showing Augmentations of honour granted:
(i) Canton to Sir Winston Churchill, Capt. of Horse, by
Charles II, and (ii) Inescutcheon of St. George and France
to John Churchill, Duke of Marlborough by Queen Anne.

Those who want to see relics of an ancient civilisation which has passed away in our own day should see Fox-Davies' book, *Armorial Families*, which went through 7 editions, the last being in 1929-30.* In every one of the many cases of modern persons having arms mentioned in this book the livery is always given. Few people in 1929 had men servants and the number now is infinitesimal, yet when Fox-Davies was in the full prime

* A reprint was published in 1970.

of his writing, about 1910, even many middle-class families kept a butler.

On clothes and on other personal possessions such as jewellery, silver, china, household tiles, arms were used. The use on silver is well known to everyone. By looking in any good second-hand jewellers one can see many examples of silver bearing the crest or the full arms of the original owner. It was and is a ready means of identifying the property. In the older examples, up to the middle or perhaps later of the 19th century

Encaustic floor tile at Tewkesbury Abbey
showing Arms of Beauchamp of
Bergavenny.

the full coat of arms is shown and these often form beautiful instances of heraldic delineation, especially when the arms are those of a peer. Towards the present century the habit of smaller illustration came in, giving us the crest cum motto form so familiar on motor-cars. In the case of small objects such as spoons the use of the crest alone was almost inevitable.

The most familiar use of Heraldry in connection with jewellery is that of the signet ring which is a direct descendant from the old use of seals mentioned in a previous chapter. The signet ring is the same means of identifying the owner or authenticator of a document, as the seal was in former times. Incidentally the seal is still used on many formal occasions as when a grant of arms is made, the seals of the Kings of Arms are appended to the document. Seals which do not hang down but which are flat on the parchment or paper are frequently used. Indeed the misuse of the Manchester City Corporation seal gave rise as we have seen to the last sitting of the Court of Chivalry. On other objects of jewellery such as watches, and bracelets, arms are often shown.

Not unnaturally arms were depicted on carriage doors in the days before motor vehicles became common. Messrs. Hoopers, the coach builders, of St. James Street, have at their works a fine collection of coach doors which bear the arms of various persons mostly royal or noble whose carriages were made or repaired by the company in the last 150 years. At the Coronation in 1953 there were a few coaches used by noblemen such as the Marquess of Bath, and on the panels, as on those of the royal coach itself could be seen the full armorial bearings of the owner. The transition to the motor-car produced two results. As motor-cars are much dearer to buy than carriages (of the smaller type) the immediate result of the disappearance of the carriage was that fewer coats of arms were seen in the streets. The second result was that when arms were used only crests and mottoes were shown. The reason for this is not quite clear as in the case of smaller cars the illustration of the complete arms can easily be made reasonably small and not ostentatious. In the case of larger cars such as Rolls-Royces owners who are peers now use in most cases only coronets on their vehicles.

An amusing story is told of a former British Ambassador to America who lived in the days when carriages and not cars were the rule. He had his carriage undergoing repairs in a coachbuilders one day when a wealthy American called in to have some adjustments made to his own vehicle. He saw the ambassador's carriage and asked what was the illustration on the side. It was explained to him that the picture was that of the ambassador's coat of arms and when he learned this the American opined that the whole thing was "mighty fine". He did not say anything more but went away to have his own carriage painted with the replica of the armorial bearings. Soon the habit spread and when the Ambassador went out he was surprised to be greeted with imitations of his arms on various carriage doors.

With the growth of writing, in more modern times of course, crests or full coats of arms were used on letter heading. This use of Heraldry has died down and only occasionally does one see nowadays the use of heraldic notepaper.

The uses of Heraldry as a form of decoration are manifold beyond those cited above. Banners, flags, and pennons, these were all used in the older days of Heraldry and the house flag lived on long afterwards and lives to-day. There are many countries which use either the coat of arms of the land or at least some of the colours of the same for their flags, and in many private families with any pretensions to property there is the use of the house flag. Firearms often have arms engraved on the butt, in the case of 17th century pistols, and it is important to know how old these arms may be and if they belonged to some eminent person because if so the value of the piece will increase. The arms are thus often the means of identification.

Heraldic china is fairly frequent in collections, but the most common use of it is in the realm of "Goss", that type of china beloved of many people 40 years ago who used to form collections of the material and show it in cabinets. This "Goss" ware was always decorated with the arms of boroughs and municipalities and was of great interest because in many cases the arms exhibited were curious hotch-potch pieces devised by some local person to suit the whims of the municipality.

In other cases too the arms of distinguished families were shown on valuable china, such as that produced at Worcester or on Staffordshire or Sèvres ware.

The reader who begins to look around with discerning eye will see innumerable examples of heraldic usage. Two other instances of great interest which occur are inn signs and the use of royal arms. In the latter instance the royal arms are frequently shown in old churches where they were placed at the Reformation as a sign of the royal supremacy over the Church. One of the best examples will be found at St. Etheldreda's, Ely Place, Holborn, a pre-Reformation church which was bought by the Roman Catholics and where the royal arms were removed from the church into the precincts as a sign that the Roman Church is under the rule of the Pope and does not acknowledge royal supremacy. Incidentally St. Etheldreda's had a very interesting collection of heraldic engravings which were placed there by one of the former officers of the College of Arms, Edward Bellasis, and which illustrate the history of his family.

Inn signs often derive from the local family who owned the land and were the landlords of the inn. They have often departed but their arms remain as a memorial of their presence. In this way some magnificent examples of heraldic art can be seen by everyone as he journeys about the country.

CHAPTER ELEVEN

STAGNATION OF HERALDRY
*in the later 17th and 18th centuries. The
position in Scotland and Ireland.*

C HAPTER Ten has been somewhat of a digression because it
was necessary to explain that the uses of Heraldry had
spread far beyond the original warlike devices employed by the
knights. In fact the language of Heraldry is an anachronism; to
talk of shields, helmets, crests, when none of these things are
actually worn or used is simply the continuance of a way of
speaking and writing which is inseparable from the employment of heraldic terms. But it must never be forgotten that the
uses of Heraldry described in the last chapter are mainly
responsible for keeping alive the science and art of coat armour.
Heraldry had ceased to fulfil its original function and had
become either ornamental or snobbish, the sign of gentility.
The idea which was propagated by A. C. Fox-Davies that the
proper definition of a gentleman is "one who has received a
grant of arms" is quite false, but it is as old as Tudor England.
The motto which appeared on the title page of Fox-Davies'
book, *Armorial Families* (see chapter 10)—*Nobiles sunt qui
arma gentilitia antecessorum suorum proferre possunt*—They
are gentlefolk who are able to show arms derived from their
ancestors—came well from the upstart Sir Edward Coke, a
man of no very eminent ancestry, who was accustomed when
making his marriage alliances to seek out pedigree as well as
fortune in his wives. The Shakespearean evidence on the
snobbery of Tudor Heraldry is well known. Instances spring to
light to anyone reading the works of the greatest of all
dramatists. It is a pretty psychological problem to be explained,
how the possessor of one of the greatest intellects in the history
of the world could have had for one of his main ambitions the
wish to write himself "gentleman". Yet such was the case.
Shakespeare was definitely a disciple, before the time, of
Fox-Davies. In the *Taming of the Shrew*, Act II, Scene I,
when Petruchio offers to cuff Katharina, she says,

So may you lose your arms;
If you strike me, you are no gentleman;
And if no gentleman, why then no arms.

To which Petruchio replies, "A Herald, Kate? Oh put me in thy books." William Shakespeare was more than willing to be put in the heralds' books. In 1599 arms were granted to William Shakespeare by the College of Arms. He had petitioned in 1596 for a coat of arms to be assigned to his father John, and the draft of the grant is dated 20 October, 1596. The arms granted were *or on a bend sable a speare or, steeled argent*. A simple coat which might have belonged to an ancient family. Shakespeare's interest in the matter may have been stirred by the possession of arms on the part of his mother's family, the Ardens, which still flourishes in the male line and is one of the few, very few English families which can be traced before the Norman Conquest. Dethick who granted arms to Shakespeare was much criticised in his own time for the type of persons to whom he granted arms. Players were not rated very highly in the Tudor period and for one of them to become a gentleman was not viewed with favour by many persons. There are large numbers of allusions to Heraldry in Shakespeare and many of these have been collected by Mr. Scott-Giles in one of his books, *Shakespearean Heraldry*.

There was enormous activity in the Tudor and early Stuart periods in the heraldic field. Although as we have seen many of the Heralds' Visitations were ignored or not fully attended, none the less the heralds did succeed in making many people take out grants of arms, and crests, and also register pedigrees. This activity was brought to an untimely end by the exit of James II from the throne, and by the failure of the Court of Chivalry to sit after 1735. As no Visitations took place and no sittings of the Court of Chivalry, the Heralds were placed in the position that no one came to them unless he wished. In the Middle Ages and right up to the reign of Charles II the heralds had had many functions. In the mediaeval battles, the heralds had been wont not only to go on missions between the armies but also to reckon up the dead according to their rank and degree. Chaucer alludes to this in the *Knight's Tale* when he says that the particular corpses were recognised "in the tass of bodies dead" by their coat armour. In *Henry V*, when the short tale of English dead is rendered, the few persons of quality are recognised and described by their arms emblazoned on surcoats and shields. But the passing of body armour did away with this heraldic function. The ambassadorial functions of the heralds lasted much longer. As late as the reign of Charles II we find them being used as ambassadors. The family of St. George (Baronets, they are still represented to-day), had as many as five Kings of Arms and some of the embassies on which these gentlemen were employed make interesting reading. Sir Henry St. George, Garter King of Arms, was sent in 1625 with William le Neve, the York Herald, to conduct Princess Henrietta Maria to England for her marriage to Charles I, for which service he received from Louis XIII of France, 1,000 French crowns. In 1627 Sir Henry was joined in a commission with Lord Spencer and Peter Young to present the insignia of the Order of the Garter to Gustavus Adolphus when the latter was made a Knight of that Order. From Gustavus Adolphus, Sir Henry St. George had an augmentation of his arms, showing the royal arms of Sweden. This by the way is an instance of a genuine augmentation, not like all those cases so dear to Americans and some Britons where the arms have been granted or augmented for saving the life of the king (the name of the monarch has usually been forgotten in the process).

Tournaments, which were also occasions on which heralds were much in evidence, had also passed away after the death of Prince Henry, the unfortunate elder son of King James I. At tournaments it was the duty of heralds to note the style and quality of the entrants and to reject any person not of gentle birth. Another duty at tournaments was that of keeping the scores of the contestants, just as in modern cricket, etc. Oswald Barron reproduced in one edition of the *Encyclopedia Britannica* an illustration of one of these old scoring cards which had been used at the Field of the Cloth of Gold in 1520. Another function of the heralds was to attend at and supervise funerals of the nobility and gentry. The arms of the deceased were borne at the funeral on banners, but the heraldic marshalling of arms and arrangement of precedence among the guests ceased at the end of the 17th century, which was a great pity, as the use of armorial ensigns in the funeral procession must have popularised the use of arms. John Bunyan (who did not belong to an armigerous family) when describing the funeral of Mr. Badman (*Life and Death of Mr. Badman*), tells us that the ensigns of the deceased were borne before the hearse like those of other men at their funerals.

Up to the end of the 17th century there are innumerable references to the use of arms in English literature, but after the gradual curtailment of the heralds' functions, the discontinuance of the Visitations, and the cessation of the Court of Chivalry and some of the more obvious uses of arms, references became fewer and some of the absurd errors on Heraldry began to creep in.

While the Officers at the Heralds' College were thus thrown back on their own resources, the Middle Ages became an object of ridicule or dislike to the cultured men of the 18th century. This did not exactly assist a proper comprehension of Heraldry. The monkish or Gothic ages were despised by the scholar and philosopher of the 18th century. David Hume wrote of the mediaeval history of England in the following terms. Speaking of Alfred the Great as one who might for virtue be "set in opposition to that of any monarch which the annals of any age or nation can present to us", Hume adds, "Fortune, alone, by throwing him into that barbarous age, deprived him of historians worthy to transmit his fame to posterity". Writing of Thomas À Becket, Hume says, "No man who enters into the genius of that age can reasonably doubt of this prelate's sincerity. The spirit of superstition was so prevalent, that it infallibly caught every careless reasoner ... the wretched literature of the times ... some faint glimmerings of common sense might sometimes pierce through the thick clouds of ignorance, or, what was worse, the illusions of perverted science." The frontispiece to Hume's first volume shows an allegorical picture of Britannia with the caption, "The state of Britain during the early period of its history. Britannia appears sunk in slavery and superstition."

Such being the opinion of the learned about the Middle Ages, it can be imagined that Heraldry deprived of several of its former supports might well fall into decay. This decay was exemplified by the truly execrable style in which arms were produced in the 18th and early 19th century. Heraldry was still maintained in the period under review because it ministered to the sense of pride and privilege as it still does, but heraldic art adapted itself as it has always done to the prejudices and tastes of the contemporary period. As the 18th-19th century style of Heraldry has not entirely died out some examples of it will be interesting.

One of the most unpleasant instances is the hideous coat of arms designed for the great Lord Nelson. His career has been symbolised in his escutcheon. The Nelsons are an ancient family, and the original coat of arms before they attained the peerage is simply a single black cross on a gold field with a red bend overall. The system of augmentations then came into force as Nelson's victories gathered momentum. On top of the red bend is placed another (of gold) which is charged with three bombs fired proper. Then a chief (used in the upper part of the shield) was granted as an honourable augmentation for Nelson's victory at the battle of the Nile. This chief is not straight but undulated having upon it "waves of the sea from which a palm tree issues between a disabled ship on the right and a battery in ruins on the left, all proper." The last two words have always seemed to me to be an expression of optimism, for surely the whole matter is heraldically very improper, though the word proper has a meaning in Heraldry somewhat different from its everyday use. "Proper" heraldically denotes that the objects are in their natural colour and style.

The tale of the Nelson horrors is not yet complete. Earl Nelson has two crests, one of which, that on the dexter, is another honourable augmentation. Here it is—"on a naval crown or the chelengh or plume of triumph presented to Horatio, Viscount Nelson by the Sultan Selim III". The second crest on the sinister and described as the family crest is something to be wondered at. "Upon waves of the sea, the stern of a Spanish man-of-war, all proper, theron inscribed San Josef (with motto over, Faith and Works)." Can anyone imagine a knight at Crecy or Poitiers carrying on his nodding crest a model of the *Cog Thomas,* the ship which carried Edward III to France, or that Sir John Chandos would have borne on his helmet the image of a Spanish galleon to commemorate the defeat of a Spanish fleet by Edward III? When Bohun dashed across the plain against Bruce before Bannockburn, would a replica of the bridge at Cambuskenneth have helped to unnerve the Scottish king? At the end of the disastrous battle of Bannockburn, when De Argentine made his famous suicide charge against the Scotch spearmen, would he have been

Viscount Nelson, Knight of the Bath.

assisted by a crest resembling the Stone of Scone? These instances are absurd enough but not more so than some of those invented in the 18th century and later.

The trouble with this type of heraldic design is that it does not merely mark a few coats but the style which it enshrines has a tendency to perpetuate itself. In recent editions of *Burke's*

Peerage there can be seen the illustrations of the arms of Viscount Montgomery and of Earl Wavell. Both these illustrations emanate from the same source—the College of Arms and its artists. The Montgomery illustration is as fine a drawing as anyone could wish, but that of Wavell embodies faults of a curious nature. The crest of Wavell is divorced from its shield and helmet as though airborne in allusion to the first Earl's interest in airborne troops. The faces and figures of the supporters (a scholar of Winchester and a soldier of the Black Watch) are distinctly amateurish. Yet both these drawings are from the same source. It only shows that the bad old heraldic influences linger on.*

While we have been considering the decay of Heraldry we have had our attention concentrated upon England, but Heraldry throughout the whole of the British Isles and indeed the whole of the English speaking nations must be mentioned for an intelligent study of the subject. It is time to turn to the Heraldry of the Celtic fringe in Wales, Scotland and Ireland.

* For further details see my *House of Wavell*.

CHAPTER TWELVE

A SHORT ACCOUNT OF WELSH, SCOTTISH AND IRISH HERALDRY

R EFERENCES often occur in old family histories to the Welsh heralds but indeed no such body of persons ever existed. Wales was from 1284 annexed to England and from 1542 was made part of England from the legislative point of view. In the royal arms there is no place given to Wales, though those who travel on British Railways may find this altered unofficially for in the coats of arms shown in some of the dining-cars the dragon of Wales occurs as one of the quarterings. Welsh heraldry was of later date than among some of the western nations, because the Welsh, like the other Celtic peoples (we call them Celts for want of a better term) in Scotland, Ireland, Cornwall, and Brittany had a civilisation quite different from that of the feudal system. Arms like other western customs such as submission to the Pope at Rome, were adopted comparatively late in history by the Celts.

The Welsh were at first quite untrammelled by any College of Arms. The mania for imitating things English led them to take out grants of arms and to welcome early Visitations, such as that of William Ballard, March King of Arms (an office which was originally that of the herald of the Earl of March, and was taken into the royal household, lasting from about 1377 to 1475). Genealogy was native to the Welsh, and formed the backbone of much of their old poetry; Heraldry was an importation from the English. The attraction of arms soon caught on, however, and writers who were independent of the College, such as Lewis Glyn Cothi (about 1430-1490), gave many armorial illustrations in their works. But despite their imitation of England and the fact that many Welshmen took out grants of arms from the English College, the great Welsh families have not taken easily to the theory that arms must be recorded at the College to be valid. Many old families have chopped and changed their arms and many still refuse to record them. The family of Madox, which is derived from a long distant ancestor, Sir Roger Puleston, has never recorded arms, but has certainly used them for centuries.

Heraldically the Welsh come under the jurisdiction of the English College of Arms in London, but in former days it was the practice for an English herald when making a Visitation which took in part of Wales, to appoint a Welsh deputy. Lewis Dwnn was probably the most celebrated of these and the pedigrees recorded by him in his Visitations are generally considered to be accurate. There were other Welsh officers who served as members of the College or as deputies. Among them were Thomas Chaloner of Chester, and Capt. Robert Chaloner, who became Lancaster Herald in 1665. Griffith Hughes, who flourished in 1639, is described by himself as "deputy to the office of Arms for North Wales". George Owen became Norroy King of Arms in 1658. "David Edwardes was appointed on August 1, 1684, by Sir Henry St. George, Clarenceux, to be his deputy herald over the six counties of Cardigan, Brecon, Radnor, Pembroke, Carmarthen and Glamorgan." (Major Francis Jones, *An Approach to Welsh Genealogy*). This David Edwardes was described as Herald for the Principality of Wales. The assistance of these Welsh heralds was very desirable and it would always be desirable to have a Welsh-speaking member of the College, but for some time no one at the College was a Welsh-speaking scholar. The result is that the College authorities have tended to look on Welsh pedigrees as something quite out of the ordinary (admittedly they often are) in the sense that nothing can be done about them. Consequently all sorts of queer things occur in Welsh pedigrees registered at the College.

To-day in Wales there is a great interest in Heraldry, and many Welsh towns, counties, institutions and persons are seeking grants of arms. More important than these manifestations, however, is the fact that the Principality has been granted an heraldic badge. A royal badge for Wales was established over 150 years ago but this has now been very honourably augmented. The design of the Badge is the Red Dragon of Wales, and by decree of Her Majesty the Queen in the Privy Council of 11 March 1953, this Badge was enclosed in a scroll carrying the words: *Y ddraig goch ddyry gychwyn* (The Welsh dragon gives the lead) in green lettering on a white background and surmounted by a royal crown. This new royal badge is to be used on all government publications relating to Wales and on letter paper of Government departments in Wales. It may also be used throughout Wales as a flag, and the

Royal Badge of Wales: augmented 1953.

flag may be seen in all its glory on many Welsh buildings including some of the old historic castles.

When we cross the Tweed we come upon a jurisdiction in Heraldry quite unlike anything else in the British Isles. Whatever may be the state of heraldic lawlessness in England, the Scot knows perfectly well that he must abide by the law in matters heraldic as in everything else. From time immemorial the Lord Lyon has been one of the Sovereign's Great Officers in Scotland and no one can tell us when he first held office. The Lord Lyon (the equivalent of Garter King of Arms in England) derives his office and functions from the High Sennachie as he was called, the royal bard of the Scottish kings, whose duty it was to recite at the Coronation of Scotch kings the tale of the monarch's ancestors. When Heraldry was invented the functions of the herald were added to those genealogical duties of the High Sennachie, who gradually came to be called Lord Lyon. There is a record of a Lyon King of Arms who was knighted at his inauguration in 1318 by King Robert the Bruce and record of the death of another about 1388. It is thus the oldest heraldic office in Britain. The Lord Lyon as responsible for genealogies and matters heraldic is a judge of the Scottish Court of Session, the equivalent of the High Court in England. As a judge the Lyon has of course the power to commit a person for contempt of court if he should disobey his orders. The judicial position of the Lord Lyon goes far to explain the orderliness of the Scottish heraldic system. The Lyon can fine and even imprison those who do not obey his rulings. This august position is backed by the force of statute law of 300 years' standing. It was the lawlessness of the Scots which brought about this highly legal and scientific system of heraldry.

In Scotland the bearing of arms began as in other feudal lands and for a long time followed a procedure similar to that elsewhere. The King instituted his own heralds as described above or rather gave the duty of herald to his royal bard. The title Lyon is derived from the lion of Scotland who is seen in the Scottish royal arms. In a troubled land like Scotland where conspiracy was always on the simmer, and the Stuart Kings met with violent ends or led wretched lives, it is not surprising that no Visitations are recorded. Yet in Scotland the practice of Heraldry was to be put upon a firmer basis than in England. The fangless lion as he is called in *Marmion* was soon to be equipped with teeth and claws. By an Act of the Scots Parliament of 1672 the authority of the Lord Lyon was established beyond cavil or argument. This Act was confirmed by an Act of the Union Parliament of 1867. Under the former

Act there was allowed a period of 3 months during which people could come in and register their arms in the Lyon's books, to matriculate as the Scottish term is. After that date the bearing of arms in Scotland was illegal unless they were matriculated with Lyon. Charges were (and are) moderate and as a consequence, there is no objection among Scotsmen to have their arms properly regulated. A matriculation lasts for the lifetime of the matriculator and for that of his eldest son—the cost of all this is about £20, though in certain circumstances a matriculation can be put through without a painting for about £13. The painting in reference is of the newly matriculated arms and in addition there is an abbreviated pedigree of the ancestry. The cost of a grant of arms in Scotland is £58 8s. 6d. which is much less than half the charge in England, but the English grant goes on to all descendants of the grantee. As matriculation is required by law, the cheap costs are a blessing and ensure that there is willingness to carry out the law's requirements.

Scottish Heraldry is conducted on a legal and scientific basis. As the law regarding heraldic ensigns has been in force for 300 years a sound body of heraldic law and practice has been built up. It is the claim of the Scottish Heralds that they are more exact than the English officers. This is largely correct for Scottish Heraldry does keep far more to the laws of Heraldry than is the case in England. This comes out strikingly in the matter of cadency. Cadency as already mentioned in an earlier chapter is simply the relationships of the younger to the senior members of a family and particularly to its head. In older days marks of cadency were used in coats of arms to distinguish the degrees of seniority. The eldest son bore a label on his arms during the lifetime of his father. The second son bore a crescent, the third a mullet (the rowel of a spur), the fourth a martlet (the heralds' bird without feet), the fifth an annulet (or small ring, pierced), the sixth a fleur-de-lis, and so on. In the *Roll of Caerlaverock* there are many examples of sons who bore the arms of their fathers differenced by the addition of a label of three points at the top of the shield. In English Heraldry the only labels on the arms which one is likely to see are in those of the royal family. The present Queen when she was Princess Elizabeth bore a label of three points argent, the centre point charged with a Tudor Rose and each of the other points with St. George's Cross; the same is true with the necessary difference marks for all the members of the royal house. But apart from these exalted cases, it is almost only in the shields of the Officers of Arms that one now sees cadency marks. Even the academic Fox-Davies remarks, "In England their use is not compulsory, but they are assumed or discarded at the pleasure of the wearer without official act of authorisation."

In Scotland the system of matriculation makes it essential that difference marks should be used to distinguish between those who are heads of families and those who are cadet branches derived from them. Only the matriculator and his eldest son can bear the arms undifferenced. The younger son has to apply to the Lord Lyon for matriculation and have his father's arms differenced before he can lawfully bear them. If he does not do so, he has no right to the arms at all. The system of matriculation is extensive, and as the family spreads through the generations, the differencing of the arms goes on. Anyone versed in heraldry can read the history of a family in the different versions of arms borne by the members. A good case of this is in the Graham window in St. Giles, Edinburgh, where the memorial to Montrose shows the branches of that great family.

The establishment of the Lyon Office consists of three Heralds, Albany, Marchmont, and Rothesay; three ordinary Pursuivants, Unicorn, Carrick, and Dingwall or Kintyre; and two Pursuivants Extraordinary, Linlithgow and Falkland. These officers are members of the Royal Household in Scotland and wear a special uniform. The arms worn on their tabards (or herald's sleeveless coat) show the lion of Scotland in the first and fourth quarters. The succession to the office of Lyon has never failed, not at least since 1452 when the holders become identifiable. Even during the troublous times of the Civil War in the 17th century, the quality and necessity of the office was recognised by Cromwell. He deposed the Lyon, Sir James Balfour of Denmilne and Kinnaird, because he had officiated at the Coronation in Scotland of Charles II; Cromwell intruded into the post first a Lyon Depute, Mr. Skene in 1655, and then Sir James Campbell, 7th Laird of Lawers in 1658. The latter·was superseded at the Restoration.

When we come to Ireland the position is as chequered as one would expect from the unhappy politics of that country. An Officer of Arms was originally placed in charge of Irish Heraldry who bore the appropriate title of Ireland King of Arms. He was instituted, so it seems, by Richard II, one of the few English sovereigns to take any interest in Ireland. Yet the Ireland King of Arms who is first mentioned in 1382 was always reckoned as a member of the English heraldic body and was referred to on one occasion by Froissart as the senior of the English Heralds. He does not appear to have done much in Ireland and the office disappears in 1487. In 1553 Edward VI created the Ulster King of Arms to have jurisdiction over Irish arms and this officer definitely did have rank equal to that of the Scottish and English Kings. Edward VI thus notes the events in his diary or journal: "Feb. 2.—There was a King of Arms made for Ireland, whose name was Ulster and his province was all Ireland, and he was the fourth King of Arms, and the first Herald of Ireland." The use of the term Ulster, a province, to denote the whole of a country is not easily explicable, except on the grounds which seem rather Hibernian than English. But there is nothing illogical in the administration of Irish heraldry. Communications in Ireland were always more difficult than in England, and the unsettled state of the country with its periodic commotions, combined with terrible roads or rather paths through the bogs and morasses, prevented any systematic Visitations. Only three are known,* those of Dublin County (1606), Dublin City (1607) and Wexford County (1618). In order to overcome this lack of heraldic inspection the Ulster Kings of Arms had authority to confirm arms which the claimant's family could show to have been used in the family for three generations. In his *Heraldry Explained* (page 24, 1925 edition), Fox-Davies said: "In Ireland there still exists the unique opportunity of obtaining a confirmation of arms upon mere proof of user. ... The present regulation is that user must be proved for at least three generations, and be proved also to have existed for one hundred years." Sir Bernard Burke, who held the office of Ulster King for nearly 40 years, in the introduction to his *General Armory*, mentions that the confirmation was accompanied by the

*But see note at end of chapter.

addition of some slight heraldic difference mark. In Ireland the system of heraldic funerals prevailed as in England but with a valuable addition, as the Irish Heralds were wont to lodge with the Ulster Office a certificate of their attendance at a funeral, setting out particulars of arms in use. These documents are useful aids to the knowledge of Irish Heraldry, but unfortunately they ceased at the end of the 17th century.

The succession of Ulster Kings continued from 1552 to 1940 when Sir Nevile Wilkinson died. Apart from the Ulster King, the establishment consisted of Athlone Pursuivant, with two Heralds of the Order of St. Patrick, under the titles of Dublin and Cork, and there was also a Cork Pursuivant of the Order. The Ulster King, during the period of English rule in Ireland was the senior member of the staff of the Lord Lieutenant of Ireland and the sole permanent member. His duties as such consisted in ordering state ceremonies and in officiating at proclamations. His office was in Dublin Castle. The tenure of the post was not broken even during the worst periods of Irish history. Cromwell appointed an Ulster in the person of Richard Carney who served until the Restoration when his place was taken by Richard St. George. When the latter resigned in 1683, Carney again held the position, jointly with George Wallis, and in 1684 was knighted. His son, Richard Carney, junior, became Ulster in 1692. With the establishment of the Irish Free State, the office continued, until the death of the existing holder, who had been appointed in 1908. Thus Sir Neville Wilkinson, who had been appointed by the Crown, continued as King of Arms for all Ireland under the Free State regime. When he died the duties of the post were carried on by the Deputy Ulster until the office was united on 31 March 1943 with that of Norroy King of Arms at the English College. It is incorrect to say the office of Ulster was abolished by the Free State Government, since it could not abolish an office created by the British Crown, but it could and did make it clear that it did not want the continuance of the office in its territory. In 1943 matters were amicably concluded; the office of Ulster King of Arms was united with that of Norroy in the English College; the Irish records were retained in Ireland, but photostat copies were made of them and these are now in the College of Arms in

London. The Irish Government then appointed its own heraldic expert, who is called the Chief Herald of Ireland. He occupies the old office of Ulster in Dublin Castle. The present Chief Herald is Mr. G. Slevin. As regards the jurisdiction of the present Ulster, this is in practice restricted to the six northern counties of Ireland. The Irish Government does not recognise partition, but while it lasts, and that may well be for ever, the jurisdiction of the Chief Herald of Ireland is in its turn restricted to the 26 counties of the South.

Each of the authorities, in North and South alike recognises the grants which the other makes. What is the position however of citizens of Eire who live in Great Britain, or what is the heraldic authority for persons of Irish descent in America, Australia, Canada, etc.? Until the removal of Ulster's office from Dublin the answer was quite simple. People of Irish descent wherever they might be living came under the heraldic authority of Ulster King of Arms. Perhaps the commonsense solution of the problem would be for those whose ancestors were of the southern counties to come under the Chief Herald of Ireland at Dublin, while those whose roots lie in the six northern counties of Ulster should go to Norroy and Ulster King in London.

It may be stated that people of English or Welsh descent wherever they live should apply to the College of Arms in London for a grant or confirmation of arms. Scots or persons of Scottish descent come under the office of the Lord Lyon in Edinburgh. This is the position of those who live in Australia, Canada, New Zealand, South Africa, etc. Grants to people living in these lands so distant from Britain are made regularly each year by the respective Kings of Arms in Scotland and in England. There are also many Americans who apply for grants and who obtain them from the British authorities. In chapter 14 we shall consider the curious reactions of this American approach to the Mother Country.

Meanwhile in rounding off the account of overseas British heraldic jurisdiction it is as well to explain the position with regard to India, and other parts of the Commonwealth. When India was part of the area governed by the British Crown, an Indian subject was expected to look to the English College for a grant of arms. There were or rather are a few Indian knights and baronets, and there is an Indian peer, Lord Sinha, whose arms were duly recorded at the Heralds' College. The position with reference to the former reigning princes of India was strange. They were originally independent princes who had acquired treaty rights with the British Crown. They were in the relationship of vassal princes whose suzerain was the King Emperor. They could not really be brought to the point of being told to obtain grants of arms, but by various ways some of the princes were induced to take out grants of arms from the College. This change was in many cases as recent as the 1911 Delhi Durbar. The Government of India was strongly opposed to the grant of arms by the College to Indian Princes. See *International Heraldry* by L. G. Pine.

In the Channel Islands many old families were wont to refuse to recognise the authority of the English College. Their argument was that the Channel Islands were part of the old Duchy of Normandy and that as such they were in a position to give rulings on Heraldry to the College rather than the reverse. The De Sausmarez family was one case in point. This well-known Channel Island family has made history in Guernsey and the other isles for centuries. On various monuments can be seen the arms of the family including their supporters. Yet when the arms have been recorded in the English College (on the occasion of the conferment of a baronetcy) the supporters have not been registered because the College would not recognise the family's right to them.

Malta possesses an ancient nobility whose prerogatives, titles and honours are a matter for the Committee of Privileges in Malta, not in London. It should seem that their arms are also a matter outside the jurisdiction of the College. In some cases, like that of Count Della Catena the arms are registered in England, but his family is that of Hornyold-Strickland, an old English family which would find it natural to register at the English College.

In the old British Empire all persons not of Scottish or Irish descent were brought under the authorities in London, in theory at least, by the fact that England is the senior partner in the British alliance.

NOTE

On Welsh Heraldry the best notes are those of Major Francis Jones, already referred to in the text, *An Approach to Welsh Genealogy*, in the *Transactions of the Honourable Society of Cymmrodorion* (1948). On Scots Heraldry there are some good and accessible books. *Simple Heraldry, Cheerfully Explained*, by Iain Moncreiffe and Don Pottinger is an excellent work which applies the strip cartoon method of illustration to Heraldry as noted earlier. This book has special sections on Scottish Heraldry and as it is written and illustrated by Scots it has a good Scottish flavour.

A learned work on the subject is *Scots Heraldry* by Sir Thomas Innes of Learney, Lord Lyon from 1945-1969. This book is of course authoritative and is also well written and well illustrated. The same author has also edited with considerable additions Frank Adams' book, *The Clans, Septs and Regiments of the Highlands of Scotland* a book which contains much Heraldry and brings out the connection between the subjects of Heraldry and Genealogy. For Irish Heraldry no specific works exist but *Intelligible Heraldry* by Sir Christopher and Adrian Lynch-Robinson, being written by Irishmen, does give many Irish examples, and does justice to the Irish point of view.

IRISH VISITATIONS

The statement on p. 111 which is derived from Sir Bernard Burke, one-time Ulster King, has now been shown to be incorrect. Information from the Chief Herald is that in 1568 there was a Visitation begun for the whole of Ireland. References occur to Visitations in Cork (1574), Limerick (1574), Swords (1572), Dublin (1572), Drogheda (1570) and Ardee (1570). There were also Visitations of Dublin begun by Daniel Molyneux in 1607 and of Wexford in 1618. But these Visitations from 1570–74 appear to have been very scanty, consisting sometimes of only one entry.

CHAPTER THIRTEEN

THE HERALDIC REVIVAL IN THE
NINETEENTH CENTURY

ALTHOUGH the 18th century was the age of the classical as opposed to the romantic and of polished civilisation as against the rudeness of monkish ages, there was gradually growing up during the 18th century the movement which was to restore a truer appreciation of things. Throughout the whole of the 1700s there was an interest in the Middle Ages which was half apologetic, half amateurish. There are examples of it in Thomson's *Castle of Indolence*, Beckford's *Vathek*, Horace Walpole's *Castle of Otranto*, the novels of Mrs. Radclyffe, and the *Reliques of Early English Poetry* of Bishop Percy. This latter compilation was the direct source of many of the works of the romantic poets and novelists. Sir Walter Scott has told us of his great absorption with the work when he was a lad and it was Bishop Percy's collection which brought Scott to make his journeys to the Border Country to gather the *Minstrelsy of the Scottish Border*. All through his writings the influence of Percy is present, with that of other collectors and 18th century romanticists. There were the poems of the boy Chatterton, the poems of Ossian and the novels of Matt Lewis. With the advent of Scott the Romantic Movement was really under way. It was quite impossible to write about things mediaeval and to maintain indefinitely the attitude which Hume had taken up. Moreover there was bound to be reaction upon Heraldry. The science began to be studied and the art to be appreciated. People were no longer content to be using heraldic emblems without a proper knowledge of them and consequently a heraldic revival began in the early 19th century. It was aided among other things by the growth of the Oxford Movement whereby some Anglican clerics began to show an interest in vestments and ceremonies in the Established Church.

Victorian Heraldry was pretty grim as we have already seen in describing examples such as the arms of Viscount Gough, but there is no sense in decrying all the heraldic activity of the

Victorian period. As in everything else which the Victorians undertook there was a very considerable achievement. It is not unfair to point out that a good deal of this was due to the work of Sir Bernard Burke. He lived from 1814 to 1892 thus spanning the bulk of the reign of Queen Victoria and was actively concerned throughout most of the time with genealogical and heraldic work in which he had become intensely interested when still a boy. His father, John Burke, often unfairly neglected, on the title pages of *Burke's Peerage*, in favour of his celebrated son, was a scion of the famous Burke family in Ireland who are descended from the De Burgos of mediaeval times. John Burke brought out the first edition of his world famous *Peerage* in 1826, dedicating the work to King William IV. It was at first a slim octavo volume, but it rapidly expanded to become a quarto and to be published annually. In addition *Burke's Commoners* or *Landed Gentry* as it was soon called was produced to include precisely those people who were not able to go into the *Peerage*. In 1848 John Burke died and Bernard Burke stepped into his place. He enormously enlarged the scope of the Burke publications until there was hardly a portion of the heraldic or genealogical field which he had not covered. There was his *Colonial Landed Gentry*, the *Extinct Baronetage*, the *Extinct Peerage, Family Records, The Vicissitudes of Families, Romance of the Aristocracy, Authorised Arms, Orders and Decorations of the World*, and many other books. In addition to all this, Sir Bernard Burke discharged the duties of his office as Ulster King of Arms. In the field of Heraldry, in particular he produced *Burke's General Armory*, which has been an invaluable work of reference ever since.

It was at the end of Sir Bernard Burke's life that the modern heraldic revival began to take effect. Four years before his death in 1892, there came out an edition of the *Register of Lee* by Oswald Barron, who was then only 20 years old. Barron was to become the greatest authority of the time on mediaeval Heraldry, but he wore his learning lightly. He had the gift of popular exposition for which many learned scholars are not famous, and was also a very considerable journalist. For over 20 years he wrote under the nome-de-plume of the Londoner in the *Evening News*. His articles showed great charm and imparted knowledge in a painless manner. He edited *The*

Ancestor, a publication which unfortunately expired in the early years of this century. He wrote in many encyclopedias and collections and his position as a great heraldic scholar was noted by his appointment to the office of Maltravers Herald Extraordinary in 1937, so that he took part in the Coronation of George VI. About the same time that Barron began to write, there appeared the first edition of *Armorial Families*, by A. C. Fox-Davies, to whom reference has been made earlier. There were to be 7 editions of this book, the last being not quite finished when the author died, and his daughter had to edit the remainder. Fox-Davies stated on his title page what were his objects: "A Complete Peerage, Baronetage, and Knightage and a Directory of some Gentlemen of Coat Armour, and being the first attempt to show which arms in use at the moment are borne by legal authority." The opening shot in the book was an article entitled, "The Abuse of Arms" in which the author became most abusive. The gist of it all was that no arms were legal unless registered with the College of Arms, a position which as has been shown earlier can only be adopted if one is prepared to shut one's eyes to the whole of mediaeval Heraldry. In order to be still more offensive, Fox-Davies had the habit of making entries in italics in his earlier editions for those persons who bore arms but who had not bowed to his favourite fetish. As the editions passed, the italicised entries became fewer and fewer and so apparently Fox-Davies scored his point. It is often pathetic to hear from people who wonder whether they can use the arms inherited from their ancestors simply because a man called Fox-Davies has given utterance to some plausible but insubstantial theories.

It should be emphasised that none of the official heralds were concerned in Fox-Davies' missionary endeavour. None the less the College benefited from the unsought support given to it.

Fox Davies' work contained great merits from the artistic point of view. The drawing of heraldic objects began to be more natural, i.e. to conform more to the style used when Heraldry was in practical use. At first the illustrations in the *Armorial Families* were made in accordance with the Petra Sancta system, whereby arms can be rendered in black and white and yet denote colours. This system was devised by an Italian herald, Sylvester Petra Sancta; gold is shown by means of dots, silver, as the ground of a shield, is rendered plain; the colours are represented by various arrangements of lines, blue, for example, by horizontal, and red by vertical lines. This system is seldom used today, and Fox-Davies soon departed from it. Many fine drawings were included in his later work, both in colour and in black and white. On the intricacies of Heraldry, as used in modern times, there is no better guide than Fox-Davies. Provided he did not lay down rulings as to the prevalence at all times of the rules which he interpreted he was a good guide to Heraldry. After all, the rules as to the use of the various charges are simply rules which have evolved over a long period. If we are to use Heraldry at all then we must have rules of usage. But it is quite another thing to say that rules which have become accepted in the 20th century have been applicable at all the preceding periods from the 12th century.

In chapter 12 I have shown how the far flung dominions which have their origin from this country have been connected with the heraldic offices of England, Scotland, and Ireland. It remains to mention the use of Heraldry in the U.S.A. After all the original 13 Colonies were purely English institutions and the influence which they have exerted on the U.S.A. has been very often to extend English culture. It is true that in modern times the pre-dominant influence in America has ceased to be Anglo-Saxon and has taken in all sorts of strains from Europe and even elsewhere. Yet Heraldry plays a part in modern America where we might not expect to find it.

CHAPTER FOURTEEN

HERALDRY IN THE UNITED STATES

IT was once the habit in heraldic books to dismiss American Heraldry in a footnote. This unrealistic attitude has nothing to commend it. In the U.S.A., Heraldry flourishes, and while many of its features are merely imitations of an English or European model, there are new developments which are in line with the mediaeval heraldic movement.

Many Americans do apply to the College of Arms (or to Lord Lyon, according to their descent) for grants of arms. At one time after the war when there was a congestion of work at Heralds' College, the *Tatler* pictured the heralds in their tabards taking part in the export drive with pedigrees and grants of arms coming down the runway for export. Certainly a cheque for £200 from an American client is not a bad thing in times when dollars are the outstanding requisite of trade. Applications for a grant usually spring from an inquiry into family history (that is one aspect of the interdependence of Heraldry and Genealogy treated in our last chapters). Americans, as much as, if not more than other folk, like to know their sources. In most great American families, and in many lesser ones, there will be a member who wants to know the derivation of his name and ancestry. To begin with he seeks among the libraries of his native city, and is often stimulated by finding an old *Burke* which gives, not infrequently, the history of a family bearing the same surname as himself. In the popular idea of genealogy all Courtenays are descended from the same stock as the Earls of Devon, all Churchills from that of the Dukes of Marlborough, Stanleys from the Earls of Derby, Agars from the Earl of Normanton, etc. Then our American begins to collect his American data. Many sources of information are open to him. The English settlers in America were interested in the keeping of records. Most of them had gone out to New England to find a freer mode of life, and as the way of self government developed, all sorts of small offices were created. The records of parishes, vestries, townships and counties in America have been preserved, together with details of land purchase, birth, marriage and death. There are also many societies which have been founded with the express object of keeping alive the ancestral connections of the Americans: societies such as those of the Sons and Daughters of the Revolution, of the Colonial Wars, of the Cincinnati, of the Mayflower Descendants, and of the Noble Knights and Dames of the Order of the Garter. There are Orders like that of the Colonial Lords of Manors in America, of the Founders and Patriots of America, and many more. Entry into these societies is by no means easy. Money alone will not get a person enrolled in these selective lists. The genealogical proofs are strict and require exact documentation. All such bodies inevitably collect genealogical information and as the purely American descent is worked out, the question arises, where exactly in the British Isles did the original immigrant come from? It is natural for the American inquirer having got so far to seek to discover the answer to this question. There is usually trouble at this point. Most of the settlers in New England were of humble stock. The fact that in some cases their surnames coincide with those of illustrious English families helps little. There are many apparently unrelated families with the same surnames. In the case of the Americans the difficulties are increased owing to the fact that while on both sides of the Atlantic records have been preserved of the settlers in the American plantations, those records often show nothing more than the age of the settler with his port of embarkation given instead of his birth place. It is like looking for the proverbial needle in a haystack to try to trace the parentage and origin of Thomas Tyrrell of London, aged 17, who sailed with Capt. Roberts in 1635 on the *Good Fortune*. If this Tyrrell cannot be connected with the famous Tyrrells of history then of course the American inquirer cannot use their arms. But by this time he has probably come upon the College of Arms and after some preliminary inquiries has found that they will grant arms to American citizens. He therefore applies for a grant and obtains one. The situation is simply similar to that of a Canadian or Australian, but with this difference. The Australian is a subject of the British Crown. The American is a citizen of an entirely independent state. In fact he is, whatever his ancestry, a foreigner. How can the citizen of one state approach the head of another state for an honour? For an approach to the College of Arms is in fact an approach to the Queen who is the Fountain of Honour.

This is a difficulty which many Americans have felt. To solve it, in a country which will not officially recognise any titles of honour or class distinctions, has been difficult but a way has been found. "There is certainly no legal reason, perhaps no reason at all, why an American gentleman should not assume *in more majorum* any new coat that pleases his fancy, but he should not assume an old coat; for if he does, he is very likely denying his own forefathers and he surely is affirming what he has no sufficient reason to believe is true." This passage occurs in the introduction by Robert Dickson Weston, Chairman of the Committee on Heraldry, to one of the Rolls of Arms, registered by the Committee on heraldry of the New England Historic Genealogical society. It expresses plain common sense. An American gentleman is a citizen of an independent state. If he wants arms and cannot prove descent from a former armigerous person (if he does, then of course he can use the arms), he can either approach the British heraldic authorities or carry on the practice of mediaeval Heraldry and assume a coat of arms for himself. The only proviso is that he should not take the arms of a family from which he cannot show descent.

Six Rolls of Arms have been issued, the first dated 1928, and the others 1932, 1936, 1940, 1946 and 1954. They are a record of coats of arms which have been registered by the Committee on Heraldry to which I have referred above. The first Roll contains an introduction by the distinguished American genealogist and scholar, G. Andrews Moriarty. There is plenty of good sense in this introduction. Mr. Moriarty recapitulates most of the instances of old heraldic practice which I have quoted earlier, and which bear on the assumption of arms to suit a man's own convenience. He points out the simplicity of early shields, the looseness in the supervision of arms and the superiority of old heraldic art—"as the architecture of Salisbury Cathedral is superior to that of Harvard's Memorial Hall." He adds, "Taking into consideration the early history of coat armour, there seems to be no reason, in this country at least, why anyone, provided he observes the simple rules of blazon and does not appropriate the arms of another, may not assume and use any coat he desires." Originally the Committee refused to register a coat of arms unless those arms had been granted and confirmed by the Heralds' College. "In view of the history of Heraldry in England, these rules were too rigid," says Mr. Moriarty. He observes that many an ancient coat was never confirmed or granted and adds that the Committee on Heraldry had finally agreed to register coats which had (i) been used from time immemorial (ii) been granted or confirmed by the College of Arms or other heraldic body and (iii) been brought over by an emigrant or first settler. This is really all a recognition and revival of the right to devise and use one's own arms. In the Third Roll, the Committee stated that it was "fully in sympathy with the statement made by Oswald Barron, the foremost living authority on heraldry, which was 'A coat is not held from the Crown, but is a piece of personal property, the right to which depends simply upon user and the right as against others upon prior assumption'."

Much good work has been done by the Committee. In 18 years well over 400 coats have been recorded and published. Each is illustrated, with shield or lozenge only (for ladies), without crest or supporters. Most arms are old and for that reason simple and clear. The Committee also assists those persons who desire to assume arms in devising suitable coats and keeps a careful record of arms of this class. There is thus a growing body of American Heraldry built on sound heraldic principles. It is a fine thing that such a movement should exist and we ought to wish it well in every way. There are, too, many examples of other American heraldry.

Apart from the arms of Americans which have been granted by authorities in Britain and those which have been entered in the Rolls of the New England Committee, there are others which are not so respectable. Advertisements are found in America which promise a person an investigation for five dollars to see if he has a coat of arms. On this being discovered the seeker is then asked for another fifteen dollars so that the arms can be sent to him. There are different charges for coloured and for black and white drawings. There are extra charges for the additional research to be made in some cases. Of course the result of the "research" is a foregone conclusion, the arms will be found provided that the requisite amount of money is forthcoming. In some cases there is an interesting attempt to tie up the inquirer's home country. For example everyone knows that Ireland has sent thousands of emigrants to the U.S.A. Obviously many of them would like to retain a sentimental connection with the old country. One such agency offered to Irish Americans a certificate of their arms and crest as authenticated by the agency concerned. The inquirer was stimulated by the information that his purchases of various heraldic insignia would help not only himself but also the land of his fathers. In other cases there are pretentious titles given to the firm or agency which is handing out the arms, but it all comes to the same thing, these arms are taken out of Burke's *General Armory* simply because the inquirer has the same name as the original owner in that book, and because he has sent his money. A ludicrous incident sometimes arises when a negro whose forbears have adopted an illustrious English, Scottish, or Irish name receives an offer of arms and pedigree.

American credulity in the matter of arms is as great as American efficiency when there has been a real study of the subject. One American millionaire whom I knew had at one time sixteen research workers employed upon his pedigree in the U.S.A., in France and in Britain. Naturally as a successful business magnate this man was not duped and refused to accept anything but the most meticulously worked out proof. No one could spoof him about his genealogy or his arms. But unfortunately there appears to be little mean between the fully documented American pedigree and that of some poor soul who has been taken in by a genealogical shark. In some cases the research has been directed by the man's wife on the ground that he is to be glorified in some way, through his ancestors if not through his own achievements. I have had some very embarrassing moments caused by the exhibition of a man's pedigree and arms by an overzealous wife.

When the American inquirer has been fooled there is nothing more ridiculous. I often acquire the tail end of such a fiasco. In one case, the inquirer had clearly been listening overmuch to an agency and had come to believe that because his name was the same as that of a peer in the British peerage, therefore he belonged to a ducal house. Another American whom I knew was extremely anxious to acquire some visible proof of his gentility and his fame. He jumped at the idea of arms and before he was asked for any money he bought £100 in dollars and sent it over for the use of the Heralds' College. Eventually he got his arms but unfortunately he had heard the phrase "armorial bearings" which he abbreviated to "bearings" and confused with some kind of mechanical device. "Send me the bearings" was his cry throughout the 11 months during which the arms grant was progressing through the College of Arms.

There is much semi-official Heraldry in America. There is the Military Order of Seven, which has a herald of its own. This herald, at that time Myles Standish Weston, was instrumental in preparing for the American magazine *Time*, a very magnificent book, *The Audience of Time presented through the curious and antique science of Heraldry*. This was a beautiful work and was an attempt to show how the reader groups of *Time* could be depicted in heraldic symbols. Although the arms had never existed save in the imagination of the compilers, they were as artistically correct as though they had been issued from the College of Arms.

Again in the U.S. Army department dealing with medals, there is a herald who advises on the significance of heraldic insignia in the medals and decorations of the U.S. Forces. This is a very sound idea because in many decorations there are details of Heraldry. The Purple Heart, an old American decoration instituted by Washington himself, and revived in the last war, for the decoration of the wounded, has the arms of George Washington, from which the flag of the United States is said to be derived.

Since this book was written a very great change has occurred in American heraldry. In my book, *The Story of Heraldry*, I entitled one of the chapters *An American College of Arms*, with reference to the work mentioned above, of the New England Historic Genealogical Society. Since that time, however, there has been brought into existence an American College of Arms, so named. This has been established in Maryland, to register, confirm or grant arms, and it is intended to include these arms in a register of American Armory. The officers of the College are: Chief Herald, Gordon M. F. Stick; Herald Marshall, Donald F. Stewart. F.A.S.; Herald Genealogist, William Henry Lloyd; and Heraldic Chancellor, Charles Francis Stein. Individuals should apply to The American College of Arms, Heralds Mews on Longdock, Harbourmaster's Building, Baltimore, Maryland, 21202, U.S.A. Corporations should apply to The College of Arms of the United States, American College of Heraldry and Arms Inc., at the same address. Arms have been granted to ex-President Lyndon Johnson, President Richard M. Nixon, and to Vice President Spiro T. Agnew.

Strongly recommended is The Augustan Society Inc. This Society is concerned not only with heraldry, but also with genealogy, orders and decorations, and all matters of chivalric interest. It issues a regular magazine and brings together all those who are interested in the above subjects from all over the world. The annual subscription is $8. The President of the Society and Editor of the Magazine is Rodney E. Hartwell, F.A.S., 945 2nd. Street, Hermosa Beach, California, 90254.

CHAPTER FIFTEEN

THE PRESENT POSITION OF HERALDRY

(i) IN BRITAIN AND THE COMMONWEALTH.

THE position to-day is that Heraldry flourishes as never before. While there may have been more day to day usage of heraldic insignia during the Middle Ages, by a small number of people, that usage was confined to a narrow area, Western Europe. To-day, Heraldry is used in the new world as well as in the old, in areas which were unknown to the mail-clad knights who first used devices on their shields. All down South America there will be found insignia in use in one form or another. It is very frequent to find that the republics of Latin America (from Mexico to the extreme south of Patagonia) use national arms, and that heraldic societies are among them. Moreover in Europe there has been such a growth in population since mediaeval times that the use of heraldic symbols is far extended beyond what was then the case.

In Britain, Heraldry has hardly ever been more flourishing. Whatever social revolutions have taken place in this country there has been no upsetting of the College of Arms in England or the Lyon Office in Scotland. The latter is guaranteed by the law of Scotland and of the United Kingdom, while the former as being part of the Sovereign's household is above political controversy. In Ireland as we have seen the ending of one heraldic appointment has led only to the institution of another.

There are still large numbers of people who apply to the heraldic authorities in Britain for arms grants; some of them being official, or nearly official persons. Peers, baronets and knights are supposed to have coats of arms and in practice most peers and baronets do have them. The expense involved, some £200 in the case of peers does not seem much as set against the other incidental expenses of a peerage. Under the 6 years' regime of Mr. (later Earl) Attlee there were many creations of Labour peers. Some of these like Lord Dukeston did not take out coats of arms but many others did. Lords Citrine, Crook,

Quibell, Kirkwood, Calvérley*, and many more had arms granted to them by Garter King, or in the case of Kirkwood by Lord Lyon. When one looks at these arms in peerage books, there is no demonstrable difference between the new arms and those of the older families. Why should there be? And why should not a new peer or baronet take out a grant of arms? The trimmings usually go with a dish.

As to knights, the number who obtain arms grants is hard to estimate, because their arms are not often illustrated in reference-books unless it be in *Burke's Landed Gentry*, and then only if they happen to come within the category of folk whose pedigrees go into that volume. But many knights are in the position that they are more or less bound to have arms. If a person is a knight of one of the orders of chivalry—the Bath, British Empire, Royal Victorian or St. Michael and St. George it is very difficult for him to avoid the use of a banner, or if this is unnecessary there may be occasions when his staff or his friends want to present him with a gift which may bear his arms; how awkward then for him not to have a coat of arms. Sheriffs also need arms grants, if they do not already possess them. The sheriff of a county must display his banner during his year of office. Sometimes it happens that a man is picked for sheriff who has been using some one else's coat of arms and then there is a tremendous flurry to provide a new grant.

But quite apart from these semi-official or official classes, there are many persons who feel the thirst for gentility coming over them strongly. A grant of arms is one of the outward expressions of the inward grace of gentle blood, and an arms grant is sought. There must be hundreds of applications in the course of one year. No one who is employed at Heralds' College is likely to have to complain of lack of work.

There are however many cases of arms which are granted to corporate bodies and not to individuals. Every so often we hear of a town or city which has put its house in order as regards

---

* In the case of Lord Calverley three ducal coronets appear in his arms. The explanation is interesting. As Mr. George Muff, Lord Calverley represented the constituency of East Hull for some 10 years. The arms of Kingston-upon-Hull are three gold coronets, one over the other upon a shield azure. They are always called locally, three crowns, and it is possible that they were included in Lord Calverley's arms in token of his association with Hull.

arms bearing. An interesting example has recently been described in a book by an heraldic writer, Col. Howard Cole's
The Story of Aldershot. In this (pages 201-204) he says: "Until
1923 the arms of the Urban District Council had been un-
official. The design which had been adopted in the 'nineties on

Arms of the Borough of Aldershot: granted 1923

the formation of the Council had been based on the name
Aldershot and could almost be classified as a rebus or pun on
the name of the town. These arms were composed of a shield
upon which was an alder tree in green and brown on a scarlet
background below three piles, each of six round shot in gold on
a dark blue background, thus linking the town's name with this
symbolism, the alder tree, and the shot, representative of the
military associations of the town." The official coat of arms

was granted in 1923 when Aldershot became a Borough and received its charter. The ancient family of Tichborne which is sometimes said to be pre-Conquest, had an association of 200 years with the manor of Aldershot, and the College of Arms granted to the new Borough a coat of arms based on the arms of the Tichbornes, "with the addition of special quarterings representative of the Bishopric of Winchester and the military associations of the Borough."

In many cases new boroughs or cities have obtained grants of arms at the beginning of their existence. In addition to such corporate bodies there are many more which have arms. Learned institutions usually do. One of the latest societies to acquire arms is the Institute of Naval Architects, and a coat of arms was granted to the Heraldry Society.

Another learned society which has received a grant of arms is the Cymmrodorion, which was founded for the encouragement of the Art, Literature and Science of Wales. It has been granted a royal charter. Its arms are interesting as an example of the allusive nature of Heraldry, ancient and modern. The shield is *quarterly or and gules having four lions passant guardant counter changed those on the dexter contourny (having face to the sinister)*. The Crest is *a dragon passant gules supporting with the dexter paw a lance or the point proper flying therefrom a pennon per fesse argent and vert*. The supporters are: *on the dexter a figure representing St. David vested in ecclesiastical robes and supporting with the exterior hand a cross-staff proper and on the sinister a figure representing an Archdruid vested also proper holding in the exterior hand a sceptre or*.

Most people who are fairly observant must know that the big banks and insurance houses have arms. The Westminster Bank in particular is fond of displaying its arms in every possible way and a very beautiful coat they form, with the representation of the Thames in the middle of the shield. A new departure is in the case of a company like Urwick Orr & Partners Ltd., who are business consultants in management. They are among the representatives in this country of a large and growing profession in the U.S.A., where the science of management has been recognised as such. Urwick Orr are rather a professional than a business concern and it is on the score of their professional standing and regard for professional etiquette that they have been accorded the privilege of a coat of arms. It must follow that many other semi-professional bodies and associations will seek to emulate them and for this reason the College of Arms were wise to give careful consideration to the application for a grant from Messrs. Urwick Orr as by agreeing they would be setting a new precedent.

Westminster Bank.

Among the clients of the College of Arms are, surprising as it may seem at first sight, the great nationalised industries of this country. One of the first actions of the heads of these great industries on becoming nationalised concerns was to have a flag and/or coat of arms. The arms of the National Coal Board were approved in 1949. The Motto adopted was—*E tenebris Lux*—(Light out of Darkness). The shield consists of a simple heraldic pattern (I am using the language of the official hand-out from the Board's Press Office) expressing symbolically the essence of coal production, the raising of the coal from beneath the surface of the ground. The heraldic description is:

Per fesse argent and sable three fusils conjoined in fesse counterchanged (it is a good idea for the reader to try to work out the heraldry of the arms without reading this description). The black triangles (to continue the official explanation) represent the coal brought to the surface. On either side of the shield are two lions, the supporters that is, to represent the Lion of Britain. Appropriately coloured black, each Lion is charged on the shoulder with a sun signifying heat, light, energy and power, the products of coal. There is no crest. The Coat of Arms of the Board is used on the Board's stationery, in the stamping of legal documents and in all publications.

Another interesting example of this new tendency in the use of Heraldry is found in the Arms of the Gas Council. The official description of these is: the coal from which gas is derived, and the flame which gas gives, are represented symbolically in the coat of arms designed for the Gas Council by the College of Arms and now approved. The motto chosen by the Council is—*In libertate consilium*— (freedom in Council).* The shield has a black ground to symbolise coal and the earth from which it comes, and flames coming out of the background represent gas. A border runs around the shield inside with 12 red annulets to represent the 12 Area Boards, the ring being an emblem of unity and each Board being a unit of its own. The supporters are two owls, emblems of Minerva, the goddess of Counsel. The crest is a dragon holding a torch to signify the Council's interest in education and research.

The most striking example of the adaptability to modern life of the ancient science of Heraldry is the grant of arms to the Atomic Energy Authority. The object of this coat was to illustrate the peaceful uses of atomic power. The supporters for instance are savage animals of typical heraldic outline, who are chained to the earth. This signifies the power of the atom which has been brought under control. There are stars on each of these animals, and the points of the stars total 92, this number denoting uranium in the table of the elements. On the shield itself there are many zig-zag lines which represent electricity developed from atomic energy. As a charge on the shield there is a pile, i.e. an inverted triangle which is an ancient and quite

* This is the official rendering by the Gas Council, though the literal sense is, "Counsel in freedom"

natural charge in Heraldry, but which in connection with
atomic energy has a peculiar appropriateness. The crest is made
up of the sun which signifies the benign power of the atom, and
on the sun is a shield in miniature thereon a bird, the latter
being taken from the arms of the late Lord Rutherford, one of

Arms of the United Kingdom Atomic Energy
Authority, 1955.

the world's most distinguished pioneers in nuclear research.
The motto is: *E Minimis Maxima*—"the most from the
smallest."

Also on the British Railways plenty of examples of heraldic
badges can be seen. In *Britain's Railway Liveries*, by Ernest
Carter, the sub-title is: Colours, Crests and Linings. By Crest
the author really means coats of arms and many are illustrated
in his book.

These examples which have been quoted are only a few of those which could be given. When I.C.I. wanted to produce a magnificent work in order to make history more lifelike to persons in schools and colleges, the means was found in *The Colour of Chivalry*. The book was beautifully illustrated by a College of Arms artist and the heraldic examples were taken from such mediaeval sources as the tomb of the Black Prince in Canterbury Cathedral.

Then again a little book on *The Arms of Cheshire* was brought out by Kelvinators Ltd., makers of refrigerators, the parent company of which is in America. The reason for this choice of subject was that the company's works are at Crewe, and so the choice of the Cheshire Boroughs was very applicable.

All these instances prove that in business life to-day there are many great concerns which not only take out arms grants themselves but which also use information about coats of arms to advertise or otherwise show forth their wares.

Outside Britain the interest in Heraldry goes in spasms to some extent but even so there are small flourishing heraldic societies throughout the Commonwealth. The arms of the different colonies and dominions are in themselves a subject of study. In many cases they have a pun in the arms or an allusion to some characteristic of the colony. Manitoba has the bison which formerly roamed the Canadian prairies. Alberta, the Rockies with the wheat fields in the plains below. British Columbia has the setting sun. Nova Scotia has the saltire of the Scottish baronets badge. In the arms of Prince Edward Island there is naturally an island. The coat of the Federated Malay States has tigers as the supporters, in the coat of Ceylon there is an elephant walking between palm trees with the mountains in the distance. In the case of Northern Rhodesia there are springboks as supporters and a pickaxe in the shield. In the short lived Federation of Central Africa, there was a new coat of arms which aimed to unite the several characteristics of the Rhodesias, North and South, as well as of Nyasaland. In the case of Southern Rhodesia there are sable antelopes as supporters and a pickaxe in the shield.

The new coat of arms was registered with the College of Arms, and had a fish eagle (a very beautiful bird) for Northern

Rhodesia as crest (of the new Federation); a leopard for
Nyasaland and a sable antelope for Southern Rhodesia as the
two supporters. In the shield there is the sun in chief, a lion in
the middle or fesse, and in base a number of wavy palets. These
three items were taken from the coats of arms of the Federation's three constituent members. The palets denote the
Victoria Falls.

Since the war a number of books have been published on
Heraldry which have met with a large response from the public,
and there are frequent illustrations of coats of arms in the
newspapers which like nothing better than to set out an arms
illustration.

Altogether the science of Heraldry and its practice as an art
have received numerous fillips in the present generation and
there is every reason to think that the interest in the subject is
more widespread than at any other time.

NOTE

One of the most interesting examples of a commercial
interest in Heraldry is to be found in the illustrative chart of
the royal arms which was drawn up at the request of the Trust
of Insurance Shares Ltd., of 30 Cornhill, E.C.3.* This shows
the development of the royal arms from the time of Richard I to
that of George V, for whose jubilee it was made. The arms of
England are thus shown from the time when three lions stood
alone, until they were joined by the lilies of France in 1340
when Edward III made his claim to be King of France. Thence
they did not change in any serious way until the Union of the
Crowns of England and Scotland in the person of James I of
England and VI of Scotland. Further changes were brought in
by the Hanoverians, but these did not last. It was, however, due
to the Hanoverian, George III, that the title of King of France
was dropped and with it the fleur-de-lis of France from the
English royal arms. No change has occurred since the accession
of Queen Victoria. It is a curious reflection that when the Court
of Chivalry sat in the Lord Chief Justice's Court in 1954-5, the
arms on the wooden frame behind the Lord Chief Justice's
chair showed the arms of Hanover because the frame had been

* Now the Save and Prosper Group.

made when the Hanoverian territory was still united to the Crown of England. In the chart, there are also sections on the badges of the various English sovereigns.

CHAPTER SIXTEEN

THE PRESENT POSITION OF HERALDRY

(ii) IN OTHER PARTS OF THE WORLD.

A s an example of what is taking place to-day in the world with regard to Heraldry, no country is more illuminating than Spain, where in 1955 an International Congress of Heraldry and Genealogy was held. Two previous Congresses had taken place, the first at Barcelona, which resulted in a proposed statute of nobility for Spain which would have become part of the legislation of that country but for the establishment of the republican regime in 1931. The second Congress was held in Rome and Naples in 1953 and it was then decided that an International Institute should be set up, to be situated in the first place in Madrid, and that the third Congress should be held there. There are many Spanish members of this Institute which is only natural considering that the Institute is situated in Spain and that the prime movers in its establishment are Spaniards. There are however many foreign members from all over the world and at the Congress in Madrid in October 1955 there were among the 300 Congressists people from all over South America, from Germany, Luxembourg, Britain, Belgium, Holland and Sweden. The importance of the Congress was underlined by the fact that it was opened by Senor Iturmendi, the Minister of Justice in the Spanish Government in the newly rebuilt University City, and that the Spanish Ambassador in Rome then took over the Presidency of the Congress. The work of the Congress was organised in seven commissions, namely, (i) Military Orders, (ii) Legislation, (iii) Heraldry, (iv) Genealogy, (v) Communications, (vi) the destination of the next Congress, and (vii) the federative or liaison commission. In such a truly international atmosphere there was plenty of opportunity for members to compare ideas and to learn of the state of affairs in Heraldry in many countries. It often happened that in the New World there was more heraldic interest than in some of the heavily socialised countries of the Old World.

In Spain a system of government flourishes which is certainly not democratic but which does lend itself to the feudalistic style of life in which Heraldry first emerged. The archives of Spain even after the destruction of the Civil War are very splendid and one or two heraldic exhibitions brought forth rich treasures of heraldic art, while on the many fine and historic buildings there were numerous examples of coats of arms. The style of European Heraldry differs from that of Britain although the basic rules are the same. If a person can read a coat of arms at all he can read it anywhere in the world, only the style varies from place to place. There are differences between the Heraldry of Scotland and of England but these are as nothing to the differences between the Heraldry of Britain and of the Continent. To give one or two examples. In the impaled coat of Sir Edward Malet, Baronet, one can see the arms of his German wife, and in her coat of arms there is the figure of a German knight or lanzknecht. This type of charge is hardly ever seen in English arms but is very frequent in German Heraldry. Again one often sees arrangements of the shield which are most peculiar to those used to the (as it seems to us) more orderly appearance of coats of arms. When the arms of Hanover were included in the British Royal shield, there was a division at the bottom of the shield below the quarterings where the Hanoverian charges were depicted. In the arms of a municipality in Spain, that of Segovia, the principal charge in the shield is also the principal object in the neighbourhood. At Segovia there is the largest Roman aqueduct in Spain and a delineation of this fills the shield of the town.

It is said by some of the Latin Americans that few books on Heraldry emanate from Spain compared to the large modern output of works in Britain which deal with various aspects of the subject, but whether this is so or not there can be no doubt about the interest taken in Heraldry among the cultured and wealthy classes of Spain. An exhibition at Segovia, the town referred to above, where splendid treasures of heraldic art were shown was the 8th. How many towns in England have ever had one such exhibition? (Yet in this connection it is pleasant to record the enterprise of the County Council of

Essex, which in 1953 issued a booklet of nearly 60 pages entitled *Heraldry in Essex*. This bore on the title page the words: "A selective catalogue of armorial pedigrees and objects in public and private custody exhibited in honour of the Coronation of Her Majesty Queen Elizabeth the Second." The exhibition contained some very valuable records of Heraldry in Essex.)

In the New World heraldry flourishes from Mexico to Cape Horn, and nowhere is this more true than in Mexico where the presence of the remains of the Mexican civilisation has inspired the heraldic scholars of that country to the belief that totemism is at the base of Heraldry. This is stated, e.g. in a treatise—*De la Armeria y su Evolucion (Heraldry and its Evolution)* by Lucas de Palacio, and with this same author one meets the familiar private family history to which reference will be made in the last chapters of this book. *(La Casa de Palacio—The House of Palacio)*.

In Brazil also a strong interest is shown in heraldry for there exists a society for the study of Heraldry which has published many useful works. It is not possible to run over the whole range of the Latin American countries or indeed of Europe but enough can be written to show the reader the vast range of Heraldry in the modern world. To turn to quite a different part of the world, Sweden, it is often thought that that country is so highly socialised that hardly any relics survive of the former heraldic greatness of the land. Indeed many Swedes are somewhat ashamed of the matter of fact worldliness of their country, but even apart from that there is still plenty of heraldic interest in Sweden. One of the principal newspapers of Sweden complained that an intellectual twilight reigned there as regards Heraldry but none the less there is in Sweden an official known as the Riksheraldiker whose task it is to draw up or examine drafts of coats of arms for new towns and also to examine coats of arms which are to be fixed on public buildings, memorials, flags, standards and coins. Upon proper application the Riksheraldiker makes drafts for private individuals of seals, stamps, etc. He makes in fact grants of arms. In former days when nobility were still created in Sweden, the Riksheraldiker granted arms or augmented them for noblemen, but since 1902 when Sven Hedin, the Central Asiatic explorer, was created a nobleman, no patents of nobility have been issued. The Swedes do not however for that reason allow their nobility to slide into oblivion. A record of Swedish nobility is kept at Riddarhuset (The House of Nobles) according to the rules laid down by the King and nobility in 1856. Some research is also done by the officials of Riddarhuset in Stockholm. The Riddarhuset is governed by a Directorate of the House of Nobles, consisting of a President and six members, appointed during each ordinary meeting of the nobility. This body exists to look after the rights of the nobility and to execute any necessary decisions. It also administers properties and funds. There are also private genealogical associations in Sweden.

The story is of course much sadder in Iron Curtain countries. In Czechoslovakia for instance there used to be a genealogical society, but this has been dissolved under the present regime. On the other hand the Communist government has not allowed any spoliation of the numerous castles of the country. Their owners have been deprived of them but the buildings are kept in good condition and used for the purpose of youth hostels, tourist centres and the like. In some beautifully produced books there are many illustrations of the emblems of the former Czech nobility. In a book on the subject which was sent to the present writer by a friend in Prague there are many coloured drawings of the arms of formerly great Czech families. The arms are brilliant in their bold colours, and some are typically continental in the charges used. The arms of the Bubnas show an impalement with on the right or a drum in blue and red and on the sinister azure a demi lion in a coronet or its tongue gules. The arms on the sinister are not by any means impossible in this country but those on the right are just as certainly not likely to be found in Britain.

Polish Heraldry is ancient and is said to be derived from the runes which were the Norse characters brought into the country by the Norsemen who turned to Poland as some of their kinsmen turned to Russia and founded the Russian monarchy. In Poland nobility was on a harsher basis than anywhere else in Europe. Titles did not anciently exist and the nobles resisted the attempt of their Kings to introduce the creation of nobility into Poland. A man to be noble had to be born noble and the only other alternative was for him to be adopted by a noble family. The Polish nobles therefore looked upon themselves as nobles *ab initio* and despised titles as the sign of those who had been created noble by a king. The original nobles were probably the leaders of the people from time immemorial and if the story of the runic origin of Polish Heraldry is true then perhaps the exclusive character of the Polish nobility is due to their being conscious that they represented a conquering Nordic stock.

The saddest lands in the modern world from the Heraldic point of view are those countries like France where monarchy has long ceased and where no one takes any official interest in Heraldry or in the keeping of records of the noble families. Yet even in such lands there are strong local or national associations which study Heraldry and try to keep it alive. There is in France the Société du Grand Armorial de France which from its offices in Paris publishes many volumes of heraldic interest and also deals with genealogical publications. In other European countries not already mentioned there are many cases of heraldic and genealogical societies. Among these countries are Austria; Belgium, where there is a monthly Revue, *Le Blazon*, and where there is an Annuaire des Families Patriciennes de Belgique; Denmark, which also publishes a regular Peerage; Finland, where there are many learned publications on the study of genealogy; Germany; Luxembourg; the Netherlands; Norway and Switzerland.

It will be noticed that among the mentions of foreign societies, reference is frequently made to both genealogical and heraldic societies. Although these subjects can be and frequently are studied separately and although it may well be convenient to have separate societies for the study of them, yet Heraldry and Genealogy are closely related and should be studied together if possible. This is the subject of the next chapter, and in this we shall see the relationship between the two subjects.

The Congress movement referred to at the beginning of this chapter has grown and progressed in a most welcome manner. Since 1955 there have been the following international meetings: in 1958 at Brussels; 1960 at Stockholm; 1962, Edinburgh; 1964, The Hague; 1966, Paris; 1968 at Berne; and a congress is projected for 1970 at Vienna. As a result of all these gatherings, it has been possible for heraldic and genealogical scholars to meet each other, to establish personal and fruitful contacts, and to learn in a much easier way than would be possible by merely reading, of the different heraldic or genealogical sources in the different countries of the world. The International Institute in Madrid maintains its position, and is a useful centre for information, particularly in connection with Latin countries.

CHAPTER SEVENTEEN

THE RUDIMENTS OF GENEALOGY
Genealogy inseparable from Heraldry.

I N the course of this work frequent reference has been made to
Genealogy, and the time has come to give the reader some
insight into the meaning of the term. It means the study of
family history, of ancestry, and of pedigree to use several terms,
which are in common usage among genealogists. At the outset
there is a curious fact in the relationship between the two
subjects. While students of Heraldry do take to Genealogy and
acquire a considerable knowledge of it, those who begin as
genealogists seldom if ever take any interest in Heraldry. This
is most unfortunate because the two subjects are necessarily
connected. We often have to refer to the use of a coat of arms
coming down from a man's ancestors. Indeed in the Heralds'
Visitations mentioned in chapter 8 nothing was more common
than to find that a claim to arms was founded upon the use of
the said arms by an ancestor. Then again in many instances we
are puzzled by the same coat of arms appearing in the case of
families who at first sight appear not to be related. The
identical arms are not always explained by a common adoption
of the same arms, as in the case of Scrope, Grosvenor and
Carminow. Often the true explanation is that the families in
question are indeed related by blood. Hankey of Fetcham Park
bore arms in which the charge was a wolf vulned (wounded) on
the shoulder, with the shield divided down the middle (per pale)
azure and gules. The arms of Lord Hankey show the same coat
but with this difference that there is a bordure wavy in
erminois running round the shield on the inside. The explanation is that there is a blood relationship between the two
families but that the peerage family descends from a bastard
son of Thomas Hankey of Fetcham Park, by a Miss Alers,
begotten over a century and a half ago. But for the genealogical
explanation we should be wondering at the similarity of arms.
But for the similarity of arms we should not even be wondering
if there were a blood relationship because we should have

nothing to guide us in the matter. Thus the two subjects are interdependent.

Genealogy is found far back in man's history. In the Old Testament there are numerous genealogies. These are obviously of the type which have been handed down by word of mouth before being committed to writing. There is no reason to suppose that such genealogies are not authentic. The modern distrust of tradition is based on the knowledge that traditions which are the product of lettered ages are at once suspect. When men are accustomed to rely upon writing, their memories suffer in strength. Traditions in the case of English families are of no real value because they are born for the most part during the time of record keeping and may well be mere inventions. I have always thought that many traditions among great English families are derived from the works of Sir Walter Scott. He invested the Middle Ages with romance and made them appeal to people. One small example is in the use of the prefix "de". This never, as on the Continent, denoted rank, like the German "von". In England or in Scotland it merely signified that the person to whom the "de" was applied was distinguished from other users of the name by living at, or possessing, property at a certain place. John de Trafford was simply John who lived at Trafford. It happened that he owned Trafford as his forebears had done before and his descendants have since, but there was nothing peculiarly privileged about the term, "de". It is used in mediaeval documents about many people who are certainly not lords of manors or knights owning estates. Yet after the time of the Waverley novels and their use of De Bracy, De Bois Guilbert, etc., it became the fashion with members of these old families to revive the use of "de" just as though it were part of their names by prescriptive right. We can soon realise this to be so by the Trafford instance, in which the use of "de" only becomes a matter of formal usage in the reign of William IV, under the influence of what people thought was the correct style used by Scott. Again it is not until almost the time of Charles Kingsley's romance, *Hereward the Wake*, that the Wake family in Lincolnshire began to use the Christian name, Hereward, because it was not until that time that they began to think of the tradition that they are descended from Hereward the Wake. In England we have had some sort of family record from the time of Domesday Book (1086) and consequently we have not had to rely upon memory to anything like the extent that the Celts of Scotland, Ireland, and Wales have had to do. To give one more example, the office of Garter King of Arms was instituted in England in 1415, by Henry V. The equivalent of the office in Scotland, that of Lord Lyon cannot be dated as to origin, but it is much older. The Lord Lyon is the representative of the High Sennachies of the old Scottish Kings who were the royal bards and who were able to recite the genealogies of the Scottish Kings by memory. In other words while the chief heraldic office in England originates in the full blaze of history the equivalent Scottish office is derived from primitive times when tradition was a living force.

Among all the great races of antiquity there are pedigrees like those entered in the Bible. They are not provided with exact dates, probably because in many cases, exact dates were not possible, owing to the lack of a proper chronology. The Greeks had their genealogies. These are mixed up with the family trees of the gods, and in most cases the divine beings are men and women who like Romulus suffered an apotheosis. Romulus, the traditional founder of Rome, suddenly vanished from the ken of his people. He was, according to the tradition, transferred to heaven and became the god Quirinus. The important thing is that the pedigrees given in such writers as Homer, Herodotus, and Pindar are not necessarily rubbish. They may be taken as genuine for the number of generations and for the names.

With the rise of Greece to civilised stature, there came the era of records. With records go two other things, criticism of tradition and forgery of sources. Once something is written there arises the possibility of corrupting it. In the case of the great Romans of the Empire, principally the Roman Emperors, it became the fashion to give them wonderful pedigrees. Thus the Emperor Vespasian, who was the son of a Sabine farmer, was told by his flatterers that his descent could be traced from the Trojan heroes and from the gods. Much the same process occurred in Elizabethan England. The great men such as Cecil, Lord Burghley, liked to think of themselves as old Norman stock. They even forged documents to prove that they were! In every literate or semi-literate country the same story can be told. There is always a fashionable source for the genealogy of the "best people". In England nearly all wish to be Normans, though a few wish to be Saxons. In ancient Rome all wished to be of Trojan descent, hence the success of Virgil's *Aeneid*, where the Trojan ancestry of the Romans is prominently featured.

In other parts of the world descent has also been a matter of great importance. In Polynesia as Thor Heyerdhal has shown in *Kon-Tiki* there are traditions which go back 1500 years and which would connect some of the islanders with the ancient Peruvians. Among the Maoris there are similar traditions which when the clan genealogies have been worked out, enable us to date the arrival of the Maoris in New Zealand within the radius of a generation of our own Norman Conquest. In China there are cases quoted (it is not known with what accuracy) of the descent of modern persons from Confucius, 65 or more generations being involved. Among the Japanese, there is the claim for the monarchy of the Mikado that it dates from 2500 B.C. It then begins in the Japanese accounts, with frankly fabulous incidents which no amount of ingenuity can fit into the scheme of modern knowledge. However there is no doubt that the history of Japan can be traced from the 7th and 8th centuries and that from a very early period there has been a line of Mikados. Here we have again a genealogy of formidable dimensions.

In India among the Rajputs in particular there are many histories of princely lines which go back for a thousand years. There is no reason to suppose that in a country of the immemorial antiquity of India records were not regarded, or that such claims are not to be trusted. [For a full account of the Rajput genealogies see the large work by Lt.-Col. James Tod, *Annals & Antiquities of Rajast'han*, 2 vols. in 1, reprinted 1950, Routledge & Kegan Paul.] The most remarkable claim to long descent is, however, that of the Emperor of Ethiopia. He is in his own view the descendant of the Queen of Sheba and King Solomon. It would be somewhat absurd to ask for proofs of this claim, but it is noticeable that in the ancient history of Ethiopia, *The Kebra Negust* or *Glory of Kings*, the tradition is known and respected 1500 years ago. This means that while the Roman Empire existed and before any of the monarchies of

Europe had begun to pule and whimper in the cradle of the earliest Middle Ages, the ruler of Ethiopia held as an article of faith his descent from the King of Israel, 1000 years B.C. If the Ethiopian claim is true, and there is nothing to show that it is impossible, then it is the longest pedigree in the world.

Genealogy has often been used for base purposes and at the behest of the rich who have thought that they might order a pedigree as they ordered a carriage or a horse. This is one of the reasons for the warnings of St. Paul to his spiritual children, Timothy and Titus, against the vain delusions of genealogy. Yet St. Paul as an orthodox Jew knew all about the genealogies of his race. In the New Testament itself we have two genealogies in St. Matthew and St. Luke, in which the human ancestry of Christ is traced. Properly used Genealogy can be a great help in the study of history. A nation is but a body of individuals and the more we know of the latter the more we shall know of the former. Nowhere is this brought out more than in the works of Sir Frank Stenton, who in his study of England before the Norman Conquest uses among his other aids to understanding the period whatever help he can get from Genealogy. He cites the example of families like the Fitz-Williams, who were derived from Godric, an Englishman, and whom we may therefore consider to have been derived from the pre-Conquest holders of land in Yorkshire. Sir Frank points out that the wasting of Yorkshire left the country unattractive to Norman settlers, so that the English such as the FitzWilliam ancestor were left in possession of their lands.

Among British people the Welsh, Scots and Irish have very often traditional genealogies which must enshrine some truth even if they are not true in all particulars. In these three cases the traditional pedigrees have this to support them, that they were recited in generation after generation with various persons standing by whose interest it was to find faults with any slips of memory. Among the Welsh the inheritance of property depended upon the proof of ancestry, because in Wales in ancient times the practice of gavelkind prevailed, whereby the property of a person was divided equally among all his sons. The same principle applied throughout all the successions of Welsh property so that it became incumbent upon a man to know his pedigree well if he wished to inherit any property.

This is why in so many Welsh pedigrees we have strings of names, such as Caradoc ap Morgan ap Rees ap Evan ap Morgan ap Hugh, etc. thus giving us in a line a pedigree of perhaps 150 years. (Ap means "son of"). It was not until 1542 that the practice of gavelkind gave way to the rule of primogeniture as it has prevailed in England. In 1542 Henry VIII, himself possessed of Welsh blood, made Wales into an administrative whole with England.

Among the Irish there has been from time immemorial—time whereof the memory runneth not to the contrary, as lawyers say—a belief in the Milesian heroes who are supposed to have come to Ireland from Spain about 1500 B.C. We know so little of the migrations of peoples in the ages before Christ that it would be unwise to dispose of this tradition as having no validity. Obviously the ancient Irish must have come into the country from somewhere, and there are evidences from archaeological research which show that there were many traces of human presence in Ireland long before the historic period. The tradition of the High King of Ireland antedates that of most of the European monarchies. Thus Niall of the Nine Hostages appears to have lived in the 4th century, and certainly when St. Patrick went on his mission in the 5th century there were kings and tribal organisations all over Ireland.

Among the Highlanders of Scotland tradition also flourishes, but not with such an antiquity as among the Irish. The great feature of Scottish (i.e. Highland) genealogy is the clan system. Clans give a feeling of genealogical depth to the clansman. A Macdonald may not be able to trace his direct ancestry beyond his great-grandfather but he feels a pride in the long line of the Macdonalds who are really not his ancestors but the ancestors of his chief. In other words the clansman takes a vicarious pride in the ancestry of the eponymous who is his chief. The clan system is such that in past times there must have been many people who were of no clan and had no status but who came under the protection of some great chief who was able to afford them the shelter which they needed in those grim days. They took his name but were not of the same blood.

Among the Lowland Scots there are fewer differences in genealogical problems from those of England. There are some clans in the Lowlands but in the majority of Lowland families the tracing of ancestry follows in broad outline the same procedure as in England. As England is likely to be of most interest to readers of this book, remembering also that in the United States there are millions of English descent, the next chapter is given up to the study of Genealogy in England.

CHAPTER EIGHTEEN

THE STUDY OF GENEALOGY IN ENGLAND

ENGLISH genealogy is distinguished from that of the Celtic races by the preference for the written record. This may be a national characteristic or it may be due to the fact that written records in considerable abundance have been produced in this country for over a thousand years. Under the Anglo-Saxons or Old English there was a considerable literature which ranged over fiction, poetry, religious writing, history and didactic works. There was little attempt to put down genealogies. Only in the case of the Kings of Wessex was a pedigree entered in the *Anglo-Saxon Chronicle*. From these sovereigns Her Majesty the Queen is in direct descent, there being 63 monarchs from Egbert (who is reckoned first King of England) to herself. In the case of the great nobles no pedigrees were written down as far as we know for the simple reason that the pedigrees of great men were recited at the feasts and festivals by bards just as they were for much longer among the Celts. It has not been found possible to piece together a pedigree outside the royal line in the period before the Conquest for more than five generations. As to the claims to pre-Conquest descent these are usually fictitious and only a very few—less than half a dozen—are genuine. The Norman Conquest, which extended from 1066 to 1072 displaced the Old English ruling class in favour of the Normans. The records such as they may have been were destroyed or lost and the written records which were produced after that time were the work of the Normans. The first substantial record, and a very remarkable one at that, was Domesday Book, so called because no dispute could be entertained with its rulings. This great volume was the work of William the Conqueror. When he had reigned in England for nearly 20 years and had finally put down all opposition, he wished to have an accurate account of the land, what it produced, who dwelt in it and who had held the land before the possessor at the time of the survey (1086). It was in fact a census, a land survey and a primitive but highly effective tax assessment. The record tells us much indirectly about the state of the various families, though of course William had no thought of genealogy when he sent round his commissioners to make the survey. The Domesday Book tells us who were the holders of land under Edward the Confessor in 1066 (Edward died on 5 January that year), and who held the land 20 years later. Most of the new holders were Normans or foreigners whom the Conqueror had brought into England. Few people can trace a descent from any of these Domesday Book tenants. For one thing, the robbers did not always agree among themselves, and so in the generation of William's sons, William II and Henry I, there were many changes among the Norman landowners themselves. Even more important, the continuity of record from which genealogical facts can be obtained was not kept up. In the reign of Henry I we do begin to have the first of the Rolls of the Pipe which give the tax assessments of the tenants of the Crown, but this is a generation after Domesday and then is interrupted again for some 30 years. In 1166 there was another Great Survey, under Henry II, to find out the increase in land values since the Domesday Book. From Henry II's reign also we can trace a regular succession of the Pipe Rolls for some centuries. The evidence as to family which can be gleaned from these sources if sparse and liable to interruption is far more valuable than many a set pedigree. It is derived from sources the producers of which were quite uninterested in framing pedigrees. Consequently any genealogical information which is given is definitely true because there was no temptation to alter it.

It follows of course that in the Middle Ages the pedigrees which can be traced are those of the greater folk. Nobles and knights, ladies and squires, these are the people whom we meet in the records. Occasionally an industrious student has been able to produce a pedigree of three or four generations for a villein, who was liable to be sold with his land. The villein's pedigree was kept by him, in the hope that he would be able to prove his freedom in a manorial court and so escape some unpleasant burdens which hung upon the unfree.

Another source of great value was in the chartularies of the monasteries. These recorded gifts to the monastery and the details of many of the benefactors. Many chartularies remain.

With the growth in the size of towns and of trade, and the breaking down of the old feudalism, the ordinary people of the land began to find a record. In 1538 Thomas Cromwell, who was the son of a Putney blacksmith and had been a soldier of fortune in Italy, became Vicar General to Henry VIII. For various reasons, Thomas Cromwell decided to imitate the practice which prevailed in various parts of the Continent. He ordered that a system of parish records should be set up throughout England and Wales. The vital statistics of baptism, marriage and burial were to be kept by the parish clergy. There was much opposition to the scheme, but it was begun and continues to the present day. At first some of the clergy showed their dislike of the whole matter by not keeping these records. In many cases the parish records begin in the 17th and not in the 16th century. Few collections really go back anywhere near the date of institution of parish records. But whatever can be said about the wisdom of the practice, or its allegedly tyrannical officer, Thomas Cromwell, there is no doubt that the parish registers are among the finest national records which have ever been produced. For 300 years they occupy the most prominent place in the apparatus by which a man could search into his ancestry. In some cases it is possible to trace a family from the Middle Ages to the present day, living in one place. This is so in the case of the Harmworths, who for more than 10 generations lived in Hampshire.

It is an astonishing thing that the parish registers have not been collected into some central place or copied so that they would be safe from destruction. Yet they remain as far as the State is concerned in the hands of the clergy. Incumbents may be good or bad or fairly good in keeping the records which they have inherited from their long dead predecessors, but the facts remain that the clergy of the Church of England have not been trained as genealogists nor is it part of their job to preserve genealogical records, and also that the hundred and one chances of everyday life may destroy the records. Fire, flood, tempest, wanton neglect and deliberate destruction are among the agencies which have removed many parish registers. Some considerable private effort has been put into trying to copy and preserve the registers, and at the Society of Genealogists in London there is a fine collection of manuscripts and typed copies of these records together with Boyd's Marriage Index which it is hoped will one day extend all over England and give the inquirer the information about marriages which he has to seek at present among many scattered parishes. There are also many printed copies of particular registers. But all this is the result of private enterprise.

At the same time that the parish registers began to be kept, a large store of other documents also started to accumulate which are of great help to the searcher. Wills have existed in England since Saxon times and some have been preserved from that time. The Church cared for wills and they came to be proved in the church courts right up until the establishment of the Probate Court (now the Probate Division of the High Court) in 1858. If a man had property in only one ecclesiastical jurisdiction, such as Exeter, his will was proved in the Archdeacon's Court at Exeter. If his property were in more than one ecclesiastical jurisdiction then the will had to be proved in the Prerogative Court of Canterbury (P.C.C.). This is a very important distinction because the P.C.C. wills have been stored in Somerset House, London, where they can be examined, but the wills proved in jurisdictions other than at Canterbury are in deposits in many different centres throughout England and Wales. Since 1858 all wills for England and Wales have been kept in Somerset House after probate. Scottish wills are in the Register House, Edinburgh.

From 1837 another great change took place in record keeping in Britain. It was then ordered that particulars of birth, marriage and death should be rendered by all concerned and deposited with Somerset House, under the care of the Registrar General. By this means everyone came to be recorded. Thus the process which began with the Domesday Book gradually worked its way down until it came to the poorest and least notable. Genealogy ceased to be a matter of property and was the concern of the State. The decision to keep these vital statistics was a natural consequence of the holding in 1801 of the first Census. The idea of this had been mooted in Parliament 50 years earlier but had been defeated by religious sentiment, the members of the House of Commons alleging that as David had been punished in the Old Testament for numbering the people so divine punishment would come upon the people of England if the Census were held. However by 1801 the Government had apparently become convinced that the divine wrath would not be incurred by a Census and one was held. It was not until 1841 that the records of the Census were kept, and not until 1851 that the exact place of birth was called for. These Census records are invaluable for the genealogist. They bridge the gap most opportunely between the parish records and the Somerset House registers. Provided one has a sound idea of where a forbear was living in 1851 it is fairly straightforward to find out where he was born. The 1841 records are also useful, but to the question of place of birth they contribute only the query, "were you born where you now (i.e. in 1841) live?" If the answer were "yes" all is well, but should the reply be negative, then all England with 14,000 parishes lies open to the searcher. From 1851 onward this difficulty has been eliminated.

The Census returns of 1841, 1851 and 1861 are available for all to see at the Public Record Office. From 1871 onwards the returns are in the keeping of Somerset House and can only be examined through the officials there. The reason for this is that the returns from that date can theoretically concern a living person and may therefore not be seen by the public.

The above is a bare sketch of the progress of genealogical knowledge in Britain but a vast amount must necessarily be left out owing to considerations of space (see the note at the end of this chapter for further information). Apart from the official sources, such as certificates of birth, census returns, wills, there are a large number of other documentary sources. Each profession has needed to keep records of its members and of those who have sought admission to its ranks. So too with educational establishments. Great public schools have preserved records of their alumni. As soon as one sees that a man has been to Eton or Harrow or some other well-known school, one knows that information about that man's parentage is available. I was once asked to provide the pedigree of a man whose name was in the news. It was a foolish request because there are not ready-made pedigrees of every person, but I happened to notice that his father had been at a great public school. This led me to the grandfather of my subject. He had been a doctor and as such was entered in various medical registers, again with details of his parentage. The parent here was a clergyman, and as in the early 19th century it was likely that a clergyman of the Church of England would have gone to either Oxford or Cambridge, I searched among the registers of those two universities. I traced him there and then found that the clergyman's father had been a country gentleman described as armigerous. Thus in the space of some 90 minutes with the help of a good library I traced five generations of the family. This illustrates the value of the type of non-official record to the genealogist. Trades as well as professions have had their records preserved and apprenticeship is a case in point. If an ancestor were apprenticed then his father's name had to be given. The City companies of the City of London also kept their records.

The great feature in all genealogical research which the inquirer needs to keep always in front of him is that he should not admit anything unless and until he can prove it. If he cannot prove the ancestry in which he believes there is no harm in his saying that he thinks there is the connection, provided that it is not stated as a categorical fact. I do not think that there would be much strife among genealogists—and there is a great deal of bitterness—if all pedigrees were given truthfully. When the necessary proof is lacking, a plain statement of what is believed or hoped is not likely to offend anyone.

Genealogical research must be conducted backward, that is it must begin with the marriage date of one's parents and so work back through their dates of birth, etc. Research so-called, which begins to work forward from some mythical stock is not worth while.

The various centres of genealogical documents need to be understood. Somerset House is the repository for the English and Welsh records of birth, marriage and death since 1837 and of wills since 1858 and of P.C.C. wills as indicated above. Also at Somerset House are various odd registers which may be extremely useful. These are records of soldiers' families, of persons born at sea, of sectarian registers (e.g. of Baptists, Methodists, etc.), going back in some cases to the 18th century.

The Public Record Office is the repository of vast quantities of records from the Middle Ages and is the bourne of all those whose searches take them into the history of great families.

Also at the P.R.O. are masses of documents such as the old army lists and the Census returns for 1841, 1851 and 1861. In fact it is very unwise for anyone to assume that his family will not figure in the P.R.O. archives.

The British Museum Library is one of the largest collections of printed books in the world and the searcher can hardly neglect it because there must in any large or important pedigree be a reference to some book which may have disappeared from everywhere in Britain except the Museum. But also in the keeping of the Museum is a fine collection of MS. books and simple MSS. Here again the resources of the Museum are invaluable in pedigree tracing.

The above sources are open to the public either without charge or else at small expense. In addition there is the College of Arms, but as the Heralds are members of the Royal Household and not civil servants or government nominees, their archives are not open to the public in the sense that anyone can go into the College and examine the records for himself. Inquiries are of course dealt with and information is passed on to the public. The normal charge for a routine inquiry is a few guineas. For extensive research the charges are correspondingly graded. The College of Arms contains the antecedents of, it is claimed, every man or woman of note in English history. Unfortunately the endowment of the College is very small (when the structure of the edifice was recently strengthened, half the sum had to be raised by private donors) and there is not enough money to provide a complete index to the whole collection. This makes the work of research none too easy. A century ago the Record Office was in much the same or rather far worse condition. It was changed by order of Parliament and by the far-sighted efforts of Sir Henry Maxwell-Lyte. Probably the best thing for the records of Heralds' College would be for the records themselves to form part of a small government department as in Somerset House, while the Heralds could continue in their present role of officials of the Household in charge of various state functions, but without the task of research being placed on their shoulders.

NOTE.

Genealogical research can only be learnt the hard way but there is a manual which can smooth out the main difficulties for the beginner. That is the present writer's book, *Trace Your Ancestors*, published by Evans Bros. (Price 5/-). In this book there are some 35,000 words and obviously there is vastly more detail there than it is possible to include in the present short chapter.

CHAPTER NINETEEN

QUESTIONS AND EXERCISES

1. What is the position when the rank of the husband is inferior to that of the wife? Whose arms should occupy the dexter side of the shield?

I N the Middle Ages this problem was solved sometimes by putting the arms of the husband on the sinister, i.e. the inferior position. It does not usually arise save in the case of a peeress in her own right who marries a commoner, or in the rare case where a Queen regnant, like Her Majesty Queen Elizabeth II marries one of her subjects, or was married to one who became a subject on her accession. The correct way to show the arms will then be to put the arms of the wife on the dexter and those of the husband on the sinister. The usual way out of the problem, especially where husband and wife are Queen and subject, is to show two shields each with the appropriate arms on them, thus laying the arms of husband and wife side by side. In the case of the last Prince Consort, Prince Albert of Saxe-Coburg, the husband of Queen Victoria and the great-great-grandfather of the Queen and the Duke of Edinburgh, the arms of the Prince were shown in a very curious manner. As this form has become familiar to many viewers of television through various programmes, it is worthy of notice. In the Prince's shield, the royal arms of Britain were shown in the first and fourth quarters, with the Prince's ancestral coat of arms in the second and third. This arrangement would have been appropriate in the case of a child of the marriage between Victoria and Albert but was quite out of place in the instance of the Queen's husband.

2. Who are the Heralds Extraordinary?

These are Officers of Arms who are appointed as their titles indicate at times when there is extraordinary interest in Heraldry. Three such Heralds were appointed before the Coronation of Queen Elizabeth II; they were Arundel Herald

Extraordinary, Dermot Morrah; Norfolk Herald Extraordinary, Hugh Stanford London; and Fitzalan Pursuivant Extraordinary, A. Colin Cole. Oswald Barron to whom reference is made in the text was appointed Maltravers Herald Extraordinary in 1937. These Heralds do not put in a day to day attendance at the College of Arms but are mainly engaged in duties in connection with the particular Coronation or other great function which led to their creation.

3. Was there ever a tax on the bearing of arms and did this give any validity to the arms borne provided that the tax was duly paid? This matter is referred to on page 82.

There was formerly a duty payable on the use of armorial bearings, but it was abolished as from 1 January, 1945, since the cost of collection was not justified by the returns. The payment of the tax conferred no validity on the arms used, e.g. if a person used the arms of the Duke of Norfolk to which he had no right, the law took no notice of the incorrect usage but merely required him to pay the tax. This is made clear from the Act of 1869 under which the amount of the tax was laid down. In this Act it is stated: "Armorial bearings means and includes any armorial bearings, crest or ensign, by whatever name the same shall be called, and whether such armorial bearing, crest or ensign shall be registered in the College of Arms or not." The amount of the tax was two guineas in the case of armorial bearings painted on carriages, or otherwise affixed to them; one guinea when the arms were used in other ways as with a signet ring. The tax was collected by the local authorities.

4. What is the real meaning of the term "Esquire" and who is entitled to use it?

The original esquires were persons who followed the banner or pennon of a knight and who served him in the capacity of personal attendants, hoping to become knights themselves in due course. By the close of the Middle Ages, the term had become a minor distinction, applicable to a small number of persons who bore no other title. In formal usage at the present time, the term Esquire is still included in the Order of

Precedence laid down by the Sovereign. At the end of this Table which is given in peerage reference works, come Esquires and then Gentlemen. An Esquire in the period from the 15th to the 19th century was usually a man of independent means who lived on his land, in fact a landed gentleman who was not a member of the peerage or baronetage. Lawyers made their way into the ranks of Esquires in the 18th century, but it is doubtful if they would whole-heartedly be admitted even now by strict purists. Doctors are certainly not admitted as Esquires by authorities such as the Officers of the College of Arms.

Apart from the usage of formality, the widening of education, and of modern commercial and political habits has made Esquire a term used for almost every man who is not to be given any other title. It has, in fact, whatever theory may say, lost all meaning to-day and bears no relationship to its original usage.

EXERCISES.

It is as well to begin with the very simple examples when one is commencing blazoning, or the description of arms. As a good start I would suggest using some of the older coats of arms given in *Burke's Peerage*, or similar works. For reasons stated in the text most old coats are fairly easy to discern and to understand. I open at random, and find St. David's, Viscount. Start with the shield. The black and white drawing in *Burke* which is all that we shall generally see, shows a lion in black on a white ground. You will also notice that the lion has a collar and a chain on him. How to begin blazon? First, the white ground is an artists' convention for denoting argent. Having found the ground you begin with the lion. What sort of lion? Rampant. (Look up any terms you are not sure of in the Glossary). Then his colour? Sable. So we begin: Argent a lion rampant sable. What of the collar and the chain? Proceeding down the lion's body we have the collar, which is said to be gorged. Then the chain. The proceeding is, argent a lion rampant sable, ducally gorged and chained or. The collar is like a duke's coronet, hence ducally gorged. The colour of the last charge, or, is not easy to get when the example is in black and white only. Still in the case of a simple example like this, you will be aware that a colour cannot be shown on a colour and therefore that on the sable lion the collar and chain must be either or or argent, and as argent is the ground of the shield, it is likely that the charge on the lion will be in gold. The next case in *Burke* is that of the St. George baronets. They have a very simple looking coat of arms which is quite hard to blazon. In the first instance if you look at the example in *Burke* you will see a clear shield (another case of argent), with a line across the top of it and over the whole a lion rampant. The line at the top marks the chief. The colour of this could not be inferred from the black and white drawing but you will find that it is azure. It would hardly be or (a metal next to a metal, and could not be argent since that is the ground of the shield and the chief would then be undistinguished. It must therefore be a colour, one of the five, and not a fur since there is no sign of the various marks of the furs). The lion rampant is slightly in breach of heraldic rules, for he must be in colour as he is not furred and is on a metal. He is gules, but part of him must cover the azure chief. The blazon then reads: argent a chief azure over all a lion rampant gules ducally crowned or,—then comes a difficult piece of blazoning. The lion is said to be armed and langued azure. Armed refers to his claws and teeth, while his tongue is langued. There is thus quite a lot of detail in what at first appears a simple coat.

St. John of Bletso has a simple coat: Argent on a chief gules, two mullets or. An equally simple coat is that of a modern peer, St. Just, who has: Gules, on a fess between three organ rests or, a mural crown gules.

Obviously the arms will be blazoned most easily when you are able to work from coloured examples. One of the most accessible to most people is the coat of arms of the Queen. Try these. You have the first and fourth quarter in the shield taken up by the arms of England. The ground of the shield is red, gules, and on it are three golden lions. What type of heraldic lions? Lions passant. They are also said to be guardant as they look towards the viewer and they are in pale which means that they are placed one on top of the other. The full blazon is therefore: Gules three lions passant guardant in pale or.

The second quarter of the royal shield is that for Scotland. Here we have the lion rampant gules. He stands on a field of gold. But note that around the shield are various lines intertwined with flowers. Here you meet the tressure of the Scottish royal house, a charge found in various other cases in Scotland. The full blazon is therefore: Or a lion rampant within a double tressure flory counter flory gules.

Ireland is relatively easy. The ground is azure with a harp or, stringed or.

There are many cases where coloured arms can be seen and the best thing to do is to start the blazoning of them. There must be mistakes at the beginning, but no amount of advice is worth the thrill of practice when you are able to make out your first blazon. Avoid as far as possible the attempt on quarterly coats (the royal arms are exceptional) at first, as they must of necessity be more difficult. If you look in most of the heraldic books to which I have referred in these pages you will find that they contain coloured illustrations and that the descriptions of these are in the text. This is a great help in blazoning as you can check your results. I do not advocate imaginary coats as these being pure fabrications for the purpose of exercise may well contain something which is not true heraldic practice.

Other books by the Same Author:
THE STORY OF HERALDRY (Charles Tuttle Co. Inc.)
TRACE YOUR ANCESTORS (Evans Bros.)
PRINCES OF WALES (Charles Tuttle Co. Inc.)
GUIDE TO TITLES (Elliot Right Way Books)
AMERICAN ORIGINS: A HANDBOOK OF
GENEALOGICAL SOURCES THROUGHOUT EUROPE
(Genealogical Book Co., U.S.A.)
THE GENEALOGIST'S ENCYCLOPEDIA
(David & Charles; Weybright & Talley, New York)
THE STORY OF TITLES (David & Charles)
INTERNATIONAL HERALDRY (David & Charles)
STORY OF SURNAMES (David & Charles)

GLOSSARY OF HERALDIC TERMS
IN COMMON USE

In the following glossary will be found not only the terms which are used in this book, but also many more which will enable the reader to carry on his studies through all the varieties of Heraldry which he is likely to encounter.

Abased: When an ordinary is placed below its usual position.

Accosted: Placed side by side.

Accrued: Come to maturity.

Achievement: A full coat of arms.

Acorned: Bearing acorns (applied to an oak tree).

Addorsed: Placed back to back.

Affrontée: Full-faced.

Agnus Dei: (Lamb of God), the Paschal Lamb (Christ) carrying a cross, and with a halo round the head.

Ailé or aislé: Winged.

Alant: A mastiff with short ears.

Allerion: An eagle without beak or feet.

Ambulant: Walking (as in passant).

Annulet: A ring, a mark of cadency.

Antique Crown: *See* **Eastern Crown.**

Appaumé: The hand open, presenting the palm.

Argent: Silver or white.

Armed: A term applied to the horns, hoofs, beaks and talons of an animal when they differ from the colour of the rest of the body.

Arrondie: Circular or rounded.

Aspersed: Sprinkled or strewed.

Attired: Of the horns of deer, when they differ from the colour of the rest of the body.

Attires: The horns of a stag or buck.

Azure: Blue.

Baillonné: When an animal holds a staff in its mouth.

Banded: Encircled with a band.

Bar: A diminutive of the fesse, and taking up one-fifth of the shield.

Barbed: A term used to describe the natural colouring of the five leaves which appear in the outside of a full blown rose.

Barnacles: An instrument used to compress the nostrils of a horse.

Baron and femme: Husband and wife.

Barrulet: Diminutive of the bar.

Barruly: Covered with ten or more barrulets.

Barry: When the field or charge is divided by horizontal lines.

Bars gemel: When two bars or barrulets are parallel to each other (Gemel-twin).

Base: Lower part of the shield.

Basilisk: An heraldic monster, like a wyvern with the head of a dragon at the end of its tail.

Basnet or **basinet:** A helmet.

Baton: A staff or cudgel which is cut at the ends instead of reaching from one side of the shield to the other.

Battlements: *See* **Embattled.**

Beacon: An iron grate or basket set on a pole, and containing fire.

Beaked: As with armed, when the beak of the bird is of a different colour from the body.

Bearing: Applied to any single charge.

Belled: Said of any creature to which bells are attached.

Bend: Two lines drawn diagonally from dexter chief to sinister base.

Bendlet: A diminutive of the bend.

Bend sinister: When the bend is drawn from the sinister chief.

Bendy: The shield covered with bends.

Bezant: The ancient gold coin of the Byzantine Empire, a round flat gold piece.

Bezantée: Semée or strewn of bezants.

Billets: Oblong squares.

Billeté: Semée of billets.

Bird bolt: A small arrow with a blunted head.

Bordered: With an edge of a different tincture.

Bordure: A border on the inside of a shield and occupying one-fifth of the shield.

Botonny (or **botonneé**): Applied to a cross whose arms resemble a trefoil.

Bouget: *See* **Water bouget.**

Bourdon: A pilgrim's staff.

Braced: Interlaced, linked together.

Brassarts: Armour for elbows and arms.

Bretessé: With battlements on both sides, one against the other.

Breys: Barnacles (*see* above).

Brigantine: A coat of mail.

Brimsey: A gadfly.

Brisure: A mark of cadency.

Burgonet: A steel cap.

Cabossed or **caboshed:** When the head of an animal is shown full-faced or looking right forward, no part of the neck being seen.

Cabrée: A horse salient or on its hind feet.

Cadency: Charges in a shield or arrangements therein to distinguish younger members or lines of a family from the senior stock.

Cadet: A younger son or other junior member of a family.

Caduceus: A wand with two snakes entwined round it, often used to denote a man of learning or of medical attainments.

Caltrap: A ball of iron with projecting strips meant to catch the feet of cavalry, as used by the Scots at Bannockburn.

Calvary, or **Passion Cross:** A plain cross mounted on three steps.

Canting arms (armes parlantes): In which there is a pun on the owner's name.

Canton: A division of one-third of the chief in the right-hand corner.

Cap of maintenance: Head gear of crimson velvet turned up with ermine, used originally by the barons in Parliament.

Caparison: Trappings of a war horse.

Carbuncle: *See* **Escarbuncle.**

Cartouche: An oval shield.

Casque: A helmet.

Castle: Usually shown with two towers, having a wall and gateway between them; sometimes with a third tower behind the gateway, then said to be triple-towered.

Cata Mountain: A wild cat shown always guardant.

Catharine wheel: An instrument of torture with iron teeth, the means of martyrdom of St. Catharine.

Celestial Crown: An eastern or antique crown with a star on each point.

Centaur: A mythological creature, the upper part man, the lower part horse.

Cercellée: *See* **recercellée.**

Chamber: A short piece of ordnance.

Champagne: A narrow piece cut off the base of a shield.

Chapeau: *See* **Cap of Maintenance.**

Chaplet: A garland of leaves and flowers.

Charge: Any figure borne on the field.

Charged: Applied to a field or bearing upon which a charge is placed.

Chaussé: Shod.

Chequy or **checky:** A field covered with small squares of alternate tinctures like a chessboard.

Cherub: Shown as an infant's head between wings.

Chess rook: The castle used in the game of chess.

Chevron: A division occupying one-third or one-fifth of the shield, like an inverted stripe in a sergeant's badge of rank.

Chevronel: A diminutive of the chevron.

Chief: The upper part of a shield.

Chimera: A mythical figure, having a maiden's face, a lion's mane and legs, a goat's body and a dragon's tail.

Chough: *See* **Cornish chough.**

Cinquefoil: A herb with five leaves.

Civic Crown: A wreath of oak leaves and acorns.

Clarion or **claricord:** By some, called the rest for a lance, but in all probability a species of musical instrument like a mouth organ.

Close: When the wings of a bird are not expanded.

Closet: A diminutive of the bar.

Cockatrice: A mythological creature with wings and legs of a fowl, and the tail of a snake.

Collared: Having a collar around the neck; also applied to a shield when ornamented with the collar or ribbon of a knightly order.

Combatant: Fighting or rampant face to face.

Compartment: The base on which a shield rests, particularly with supporters.

Componé, compony: When a single row of rectangular pieces is made up of alternate tinctures. *See* **counter componé.**

Confronté: Facing each other.

Conjoined: United.

Conjoined in lure: Applied to two wings joined together with their tips downwards.

Contourné: When an animal faces the sinister side of the shield.

Corbie: A raven (cf. the well-known surname Corbet which means raven).

Corded: A charge bound with cords.

Cornish Chough: A crow with red or yellowish beak and legs.

Coronets: Used for princes or peers.

Cotise: A diminutive of the bend, usually borne in pairs, with a charge between them.

Cotised: Placed between two cotises. On either side of a fesse or bend are described as a fesse etc. cotised.

Couchant: Lying down with head uplifted.

Couché: A shield suspended by one corner from a belt.

Counter changed: Where a field is divided per bend etc., and the charges in each section are of the tincture of the field in the other section.

Counter embattled: (*See* **Embattled**) when the charge is marked with battlements on each side.

Counter embowed: Bent in the reverse direction.

Counter Flory: A tressure flory, in which the alternate fleurs de lis are reversed.

Counter vair: *See* **Vair,** from which it differs in that the bells of the same colour are arranged base to base and point to point.

Couped: Cut off by a straight line (contrast erased), app[ied to the head or limbs of an animal.

Couple close: Diminutive of a chevronel, always borne in pairs.

Courant: Running.

Coward: An animal shown with its tail between its legs.

Cramp: A piece of iron, usually borne in couples and turned up at each end.

Crampons: Hooks used in building.

Crenellée: *See* **Embattled.**

Crest: Object shown on top of the helmet.

Crest coronet: The small crown from which a crest rises.

Crested: When the crest or comb of a cock or cockatrice is of a different tincture to the rest of the body.

Crined: When the beard or hair of an object differs in tincture from the body.

Cronel: The blunted head of a tilting spear.

Cross: Probably the most extensively used of all heraldic devices.

Crozier: A prelate's staff, used by archbishops, bishops, abbots etc.

Crusily: When the field is charged with crosses.

Cubit-arm: The hand and arm cut off at the elbow.

Cuisses: Armour covering thighs and knees.

Dancetté: When lines of which the teeth or indents are larger or wider than those of the line indented.

Debruised: When an ordinary such as a bend, is placed across another charge.

Dechaussé: *See* **Dismembered** or **Demembered.**

Decked: When the feathers of a bird are trimmed at the edges with a tincture different from the rest of the body.

Decrescent: When the moon is in its last quarter, with the horns turned towards the sinister side of the shield.

Defamed: When an animal is shown minus its tail.

Degrees: Having steps at the base, as of a cross calvary, hence degraded.

Dejected: Anything thrown down.

Demi: Half, applied to head or top unless otherwise stated.

Despectant: An animal looking down.

Dexter: Right hand, it must always be understood that a shield is supposed to be held by someone, hence the right of the shield corresponds to the viewer's left hand.

Diapered: A covering of floral-type enrichment, where the colour differs from that of the rest of the charge.

Differenced: Implies brisures or marks of cadency.

Dimidiated: Divided into two equal parts.

Disclosed: Wings expanded, of tame birds.

Dismembered, or **demembered:** When an animal or other charge has portions severed from it, and set at a little distance from each other, yet still keeping the outline of the figure.

Displayed: Wings extended, of birds of prey.

Disponed: Arranged.

Distilling: Letting fall drops of blood.

Dormant: Sleeping (of an animal) but with the head resting on the forepaws; contrast couchant.

Double queued: Having two tails.

Double tressure: One tressure within another.

Doubled: When a lambrequin is lined of a different tincture.

Dovetailed: In form of wedges.

Dragon: A mythical monster, shown as a quadruped in English heraldry.

Drawing iron: An instrument used by wiredrawers.

Ducal coronet: Really the same as crest coronet, composed of four leaves all of the same height above the rim.

Eastern Crown: A band of gold from which rise pointed rays.

Eclipsed: Said of the sun when shown in red or black tincture.

Eft: A newt.

Eight foil: An eight-leaved grass.

Elevated: Of wings raised above the head.

Embattled: Battlements as of a fortress; *see also* counter-embattled.

Embowed: Bowed or bent.

Embrued: Stained with drops of blood.

Endorse: A diminutive of the pale.

Endorsed: *See* **Addorsed.**

Enfield: A mythological animal, with the head of a fox, legs of an eagle, body and hind legs of a greyhound, and the tail of a lion. Very rare, but the crest of the O'Kelly family.

Enfiled: When a charge is pierced by the blade of a sword or other weapon.

Engoulant: Devouring.

Engoulé: When a charge has its end in the mouth of an animal.

Engrailed: A partition line scalloped.

Enhanced: When an ordinary is placed above its usual position.

Enmanche: *See* **Manche,** a sleeve.

Ensigned: When a charge has another placed above, or is 'adorned' with it.

Enté: Grafted.

Enté en Pointe: A division of the shield which rises from base towards fesse point. Used in Continental heraldry.

Environed: Surrounded.

Epaulier: Armour used on the shoulder.

Equipped: A horse fully armed and provided with trappings.

Eradicated: When trees are shown torn up by the roots.

Erased: In contrast to couped, means forcibly torn off the body, leaving the severed part jagged.

Erect: Upright.

Ermine: White fur with black spots.

Ermines: Black fur with white spots.

Erminois: Gold fur with black spots.

Escallop shell: The well-known badge of the pilgrims to the Holy Land or other shrines.

Escarbuncle: A charge derived from the iron bands which radiated from the boss of a shield and helped to strengthen it.

Escutcheon: Shield.

Escutcheon of pretence: A small shield placed in the middle of a man's shield and bearing upon it the arms of his wife, when the latter is an heraldic heiress.

Esquire: A term applied to a form of the gyron.

Estoile: A star with six points, whereas a mullet has five.

Evett, or **Lizard:** A small creature like a miniature crocodile.

Expanded: Opened or displayed.

Falchion: A broadsword.

False: Voided (qv).

Fan: A winnowing instrument for blowing away chaff.

Feathered: Arrows which have wings different in tincture from the shaft. *See also* **Flighted.**

Fer-de-Fourchette: When crosses end in a forked iron.

Fer-de-moline: A millrind, ie, the iron fixed in the middle of a millstone.

Fermail: The buckle of a belt.

Fesse: An ordinary formed by two horizontal lines across shield, taking up one-third of the area.

Fessepoint: Centre of the shield.

Fessewise: Placed in the direction of a fesse.

Fettered: *See* **Spancelled.**

Fetter lock: A shackle with a lock.

Field: Surface of the shield on which charges may be borne.

Figured: When the sun or other objects have a human face.

File: Label (qv).

Fillet: A diminutive of the chief.

Fimbriated: A narrow bordure with a different tincture.

Fireball: A grenade or bomb with flames coming from the top.

Firme: Applied to a cross patée when it extends to the edge of the escutcheon.

Finned: When the teeth, tail and fins (eg, of a whale) are tinctured gules.

Fitchée: Pointed at end, to fix in ground.

Flanches or **Flaunches:** When the shield has on both sides a segment of a circle drawn from chief to base.

Flanks: Sides of the shield.

Fleece: The badge of the Order of the Golden Fleece; a sheep suspended by the middle.

Fleuretty: A surface semé of fleur-de-lis.

Fleur de lis: Flower of the lily, the heraldic variety of which has three leaves only

Fleury: Ornamented with fleur-de-lis.

Flexed: Bent or bowed.

Flighted: *See* **Feathered.**

Flory, Floretty = **Fleuretty.**

Flotant: Floating.

Flowered: Used of plants when they show their flowers.

Foliated: Leaved.

Formée: Pattée.

Fountain: A roundle wavy argent and azure.

Fourchée: Forked.

Fracted: Broken.

Fraise: A strawberry-leaf, in Scotland a cinquefoil.

Fresnée: Rearing or standing on the hind legs.

Fret: An ordinary.

Fretty: When a field is covered with frets.

Fructed: Fruited, bearing fruit.

Fumant: Emitting smoke.

Furnished: Equipped as of a horse with saddle, bridle etc.

Fusil: A narrow lozenge.

Fusilly: Covered with fusils.

Gads: Plates of steel and iron.

Galley: Ship driven with sails and oars; *see also* **Lymphad.**

Gamb: The whole foreleg of a beast, as apart from a paw, which is shown as couped or erased from the middle joint.

Garb: A wheatsheaf, or if of other grain, the kind must be specified.

Gardant: Guardant, full-faced.

Gardebras: Armour covering the elbows.

Garde-visure: The visor of a helmet.

Garland: A wreath of leaves or flowers.

Garnished: Ornamented.

Gauntlet: A steel glove.

Gaze, at: An animal of the chase, when looking full front.

Gemell: *See* **Bars gemel.**

Genet: A small animal like a weasel or a fox.

Gerated: Differenced by small charges.

Geratting: The process of such differencing.

Gillyflower: A blood-red carnation.

Giron: *See* **Gyron.**

Girt, Girded: Bound round with a band.

Gliding: Applied to snakes moving fesseways.

Glory: Rays surrounding a charge.

Gobony: *See* **Compony.**

Gonfanon or **Gonfalon:** A standard.

Gorge, or **Gurge:** A water bouget.

Gorged: Wearing a collar.

Gorges: A whirlpool (the punning coat of a famous family of that name, Gorges).

Gorget: Breast armour.

Goutte: A drop.

Gouttée. Guttée: Semé of drops.

Gradient: As of a tortoise walking.

Greaves: Armour for the legs.

Grice: A young wild boar.

Grieces: Steps.

Griffin, or **Gryphon:** A mythical animal, the upper half an eagle, the lower a lion. The male version has no wings.

Gringolée: Crosses whose ends are the heads of serpents.

Guardant: Full-faced.

Guidon: A pennon or flag.

Guiuré: Gringolé.

Gules: Red.

Guttée: Semé of drops, as of water (d'eau), of blood (de sang) etc.

Gyron: Lower half of a quarter formed by a diagonal line.

Gyronny: The division of the shield by cross and saltire, in parts from six to twelve. The well-known coat of the Campbells, the Dukes of Argyll is gyronny of eight, or and sable.

Habergeon: A coat of mail without sleeves.

Habited: Clothed.

Haie: A hedge.

Handled: Applicable to spears.

Harpy: A fabulous creature, a bird with a virgin's face, neck and breasts, and the body and legs of a vulture.

Hart: A stag in its sixth year.

Harvest fly: A butterfly.

Hatchment: The representation of a person's arms formerly placed on his house after his death. Often found in old churches in England.

Hauberk: A coat of chain mail armour.

Hauriant: When a fish is shown in the perpendicular position, as if sucking in air.

Haussé: Enchanted.

Hawk's bells and jesses: The latter being the thongs which fastened the bells to the hawk's legs.

Hawk's lure: Made up of two wings conjoined with the tips downwards, with a line attached ending in a ring. Wings thus shown are said to be in lure or conjoined in lure.

Hay fork: *See* **Shake fork.**

Heads: Shown in profile unless otherwise stated.

Hempbreak: Hackle.

Hillock: In heraldry, denotes more than one hill.

Hilted: The hilt of a sword when its tincture differs from that of the blade.

Hind: The female deer, usually shown as trippant (tripping).

Hirondelle: A swallow.

Hood: Coif or hood of a monk.

Hooded: Said of the human face when the headdress is of a different tincture; also of a hawk when the latter wears a hood or mask, as in falconry.

Hoofed: When the hoofs are of a different tincture.

Horned: When the horns are of a different tincture.

Humetté: When an ordinary is couped so that it does not touch the sides of the shield.

Hurst: A clump of trees.

Hurt: An azure roundel.

Hurtée: Charged, or semé with hurts.

Hydra: A fabulous many-headed dragon.

Ibex: An animal with straight horns (in British armory).

Imbrued: Emdrued.

Impaled: Two coats in the same shield in pale.

Imperial Crown: Much the same as a regal crown. Imperially Crowned, when the charge etc. is thus crowned.

In lure: Hawk's lure.

In pride: Said of a peacock having its tail expanded.

In splendour: When the sun is surrounded by rays.

Incensed: When animals have flames issuing from mouth and ears.

Indented: A line having small indentations (contrast dancettée).

Inescutcheon: Escutcheon of pretence.

Ink moline: A mill rind.

Invected: Similar to engrailed but with spikes pointing inwards instead of outwards.

Issuant: Rising out of. When said of an animal, only the upper half of the animal is shown.

Jellop: The comb of a cock; hence 'jelloped'.

Jessant: Shooting forth; only half of the charge is shown when blazoned thus.

Jessant de lis: A leopard's face with fleur-de-lis passing through the mouth.

Joinant: Conjoined.

Jupon: A surcoat.

Knotted: Said of trees.

Knowed: *See* **Nowed.**

Label: A cadency mark, a rectangular piece having three pendants.

Ladder, scaling: A ladder with hooks, used in sieges.

Lamb, Pascal: *See* **Agnus Dei.**

Lambrequin: Mantling.

Langued: When the tongue of an animal is of a different tincture.

Larmes: Tears.

Lattice: Trellis.

Laver: A cutter, or ploughshare.

Legged: When the legs of a bird are of a different tincture.

Leopards: In French heraldry the same as a lion, passant guardant, hence the former blazoning of the royal lions of England as leopards.

Leopard's face: When the head is represented affrontée or guardant, and no part of the neck is visible.

Leopard's head: When the head is in profile or affrontée if part of the neck is visible.

Lever: A cormorant.

Lined: When the inside lining of a mantle etc. is of a different tincture.

Lioncel: A young lion.

Lion poisson (sealion): A mythical creature, a lion in the upper half, fish in the lower.

Liston: Scroll of the mottoe.

Lodged: When the stag etc. is lying on the ground or at rest.

Lozenge: A charge shaped like a diamond and four-sided.

Lozengy: Covered with lozenges.

Lucy, or **Luce:** A pike fish.

Lure: *See* **Hawk's lure.**

Lymphad: A gallery.

Maiden's head: The head and neck of a woman couped below the breast, the head wreathed with roses, and crowned with an antique crown.

Manch or **Maunch:** A sleeve.

Manchet: A cake of bread.

Maned: When the mane is of a different tincture.

Martlet: A bird without feet, otherwise a martin or swallow, with tufts of feathers where the legs join the body.

Mascle: A voided lozenge.

Masculy: Covered with mascles.

Masoned, or **Massonné:** A division by lines to depict the mortar between the stones of buildings.

Membered: When the beak and legs of a bird are of a different tincture.

Merlion: A martlet.

Merlé: Mingled.

Metals: Or and argent.

Millrind: Fer de Moline.

Mort: A death's head or skull.

Moor's Head: Head of a negro in profile, couped at the neck, wreathed about the temples.

Morion: A steel cap.

Morné or **Mortné:** A lion without tongue, teeth or claws.

Morse: A sea lion.

Mound: An orb or globe (of the world) denoting sovereignty.

Mount: When a hill is shown in the base of the shield.

Mounted: When a horse bearing a rider is shown.

Mounting: Animals of the chase shown in the same position as an animal of prey—which is rampant.

Mourné: Mourned, blunted.

Mullet: A star of five points.

Mullet pierced: A mullet which is pierced in the centre, like the rowel of a spur.

Muraillé: Walled.

Mural crown: A coronet of gold.

Murrey: The colour sanguine.

Muzzled: When a bear or other animal has its mouth tied with bands.

Naiant: Swimming, as of fish shown horizontally.

Naissant: Rising or coming out of the middle of an ordinary.

Narcissus: A flower of six petals.

Naval crown: A gold coronet composed of sterns and sails of ships on the upper edge.

Nebulée or **Nebuly:** A line of partition.

Newed: When the fibres of leaves and plants are of a different tincture.

Newt: An effet or eft.

Nislée or **nillé:** Formed of slender or narrow lines.

Nombril: A point in a shield last but one from the base.

Nowed: knotted, said of the tails of serpents.

Ombré: Shaded.

Ondé, Undy or **Undée:** Wavy.

Opinicus: Mythical creature, with a lion's legs, eagle's head and neck, with wings and a short tail.

Oppressed: *See* **Debruised.**

Or: The metal gold.

Orb: *See* **Mound.**

Ordinary: Some heraldic charges very frequently used. Called honourable ordinaries.

Ordinaries. Sub-: Charges also frequently used but of lesser importance than the ordinaries.

Oreiller: A cushion.

Organ rest: A clarion (qv).

Orle: A narrow bordure, but detached from the edge of the shield; charges said to be in orle are arranged in this manner.

Orlé: Bordered.

Ounce: A lynx, the upper part of the animal is tawny white, the lower of an ash colour, over all there is a sprinkling of black dots.

Overall: When a charge is placed over all other bearings.

Overt: Open, as with birds having wings open for taking flight.

Owl: Always shown full-faced.

Pale: An ordinary, a band placed vertically in the centre of a shield.

Palisado Crown: A gold coronet oranmented with golden palisades on the upper rim.

Palisse: A division of the field by piles, meant to give the appearance of palisades.

Pall, or **Pallium:** An archiepiscopal vestment made of white lamb's wool, in the shape of the letter Y, bearing five crosses patées fitchées.

Pallet: A diminutive of the pale.

Paly: Divided into perpendicular divisions like pales with alternate tinctures and the number of such divisions must be given as paly of six etc.

Paly bendy: Divided into lozenge shapes by lines paleways and bendways.

Palmer's staff: A pilgrim's staff.

Panther: A wild animal shown with fire issuing from mouth and ears.

Papilonné: A form of the fur vair, but covered with scales like a butterfly's wings.

Party per bend etc.: Said when the field or charge is divided by a line drawn in the direction of the particular ordinary.

Paschal Lamb: Agnus Dei.

Passant: When an animal is walking and looking straight before it.

Passant guardant: Said of a beast walking but full-faced (affrontée).

M

Passant reguardant: Walking but looking backwards.

Passion Cross: Differs from the Calvary Cross (qv) in not having steps.

Passion nail: A long spike with a rectangular head.

Pattes: Paws of a beast.

Patonce: A floiated form of the cross.

Patty, Patée: A cross with each arm expanding from the centre and ending in a straight line.

Pavilion: A tent; also the canopy under which the arms of a sovereign are shown.

Pean: A fur, like ermine but with sable ground and golden spots.

Peel: An instrument used by bakers for drawing bread out of an oven.

Pegasus: A mythical winged horse.

Pelican: Represented usually with wings, expanded and vulning her breast from which drops of blood are falling. When she feeds her young in this way, she is said to be 'in her piety'.

Pellet: A sable roundel.

Pelletty: A semé of pellets.

Pennon: An oblong flag.

Pennoncel: A small flag.

Penny-yard-penny: A silver coin.

Per: *See* **Party.**

Perforated: Voided or pierced.

Petionel: A pistol.

Pheon: The head of an arrow or dart.

Phoenix: A mythical bird, rising from flames.

Pierced: When a charge is perforated so as to show the field.

Piety: *See* **Pelican.**

Pile: One of the ordinaries.

Pilgrim's scrip: A wallet, or bag.

Plate: A flat silver roundel.

Playing tables: Backgammon boards.

Plenitude: Applied to the moon when full.

Ployé: Bent or curved.

Poing: The hand closed (appaumé = open).

Point, in: When piles, swords etc. are arranged as approaching each other in the base of the shield.

Pomegranate: A foreign fruit. The blazon must always state that it is slipped, leaved or seeded.

Pomme: A green roundel, pl. pomies.

Pommelly or **Pommetty:** Of a cross whose arms end in balls.

Popinjay: A parrot.

Portcullis: The grating closing a fortress gate, usually shown with spikes in the base and chains attached to its upper beam.

Posed: Statant.

Potent: (i) A crutch, (ii) a fur made of crutch or T-shaped divisions.

Pouldron: Armour for the shoulder.

Pounce: Talons of a bird of prey.

Powdered: Semé.

Prester John: Erroneous description of the figure of Christ.

Pretence, Escutcheon of: The small shield borne in the middle of a shield to denote the arms of an heiress.

Pride, in its: Applied to peacock etc. with tail expanded.

Proper: Borne in its natural colour.

Purfled: Bordered.

Purpure: Purple.

Pyot: A magpie.

Quarter: A sub ordinary.

Quartered: Divided into quarters.

Quarterings: Different coats combined into one shield, more than four in many cases.

Quarterly: When the shield is divided into four equal sections by lines.

Quatrefoil: A herb with four leaves.

Queue: The tail of an animal.

Queue fourchée: Double queued (qv).

Quise, a la: At the thigh.

Radiant: Shining with rays.

Raguly: Used of a line or partition, the projections being oblique. It can be described also as like the stem of a tree from which the branches have been cut.

Ramé: Branched or attired.

Rampant: W en an animal is shown standing erect on its hind legs, as with the lion rampant of Scotland.

Rampant guardant: Standing on the hind legs but with face affrontée.

Rampant reguardant: Standing on hind legs with the head looking backwards.

Rampant sejant: Sitting in profile with the forelegs raised.

Rangé: Arranged in order.

Ravissant: When a beast of prey is carrying its victim in its jaws.

Rayonnant: Adorned with beams of light.

Rays of the sun: Sixteen in number, nine round an estoile.

Razed: *See* **Erased.**

Rebated: When a portion of the end is removed.

Rebus: Similar to a canting coat, when the charges allude to the bearer's name.

Reclinant: Bending backwards.

Recontre: *See* **Cabossed.**

Reflexed or **Reflected:** Bent back.

Reguardant: Looking backward.

Reindeer: A stag with double attires.

Remora: A serpent.

Removed: When an ordinary has fallen or been taken from its proper position.

Renverse: When anything is shown contrary to its natural position.

Rere-mouse: A bat.

Respectant, or **Respecting:** When animals are shown face to face.

Reserved: Contrary to usual positions.

Rest: *See* **Clarion.**

Retorted: Bent or twisted back, as serpents are shown wreathed one in another.

Retranché: Again divided in a bend, cf, recoupé when in a field divided per fesse, a piece is again divided per fesse.

Reversed: Turned upside down.

Riband: A diminutive of the bendlet.

Rising: When birds are shown as if preparing for flight.

Rompu, Rompé: Broken.

Rose: Always shown as full blown, the petals expanded, seeded in the middle with five green barbs or leaves behind them. An heraldic red rose is blazoned gules, not proper. The terms 'barbed' and 'seeded proper' mean that the barbs are green and the seeds yellow.

Roundles: Sub-ordinaries.

Rousant: Rising, said of a bird preparing to fly.

Rustre: A lozenge with a circular piercing.

Sable: Black.

Sagittarius or **Sagittary:** A centaur (qv) with bow and arrows.

Salamander: A mythical animal, supposed to be born in fire; shown as green surrounded by flames.

Saliant: Leaping.

Salmon spear: A harpoon.

Saltant: When an animal is shown as springing forward.

Saltire: The ordinary formed like an 'X'.

Saltirewise or **Saltireways:** In the form of a saltire.

Saltorels: Small saltires.

Sanglant: Bloody, torn off.

Sanglier: A wild boar.

Sanguine: Blood colour (or murrey).

Saracen's head: Same as a moor's head (qv).

Sarcellée: Cut through in the middle.

Satyr: A mythical creature, half antelope, half man.

Scallop: A shell.

Scarpe: A diminutive of the bend sinister.

Scintillant: Sparkling.

Scorpion: Resembles a crayfish and is shown erect.

Scrip: A pilgrim's purse.

Scruttle: A winnowing fan.

Seadog: Drawn like a seal but with a beaver's tail, a finned crest along the whole back, the legs scaled and the feet webbed.

Sea horse: A mythical creature, the forepart and head resembling a horse with webbed feet, and the hind part having a fish's tail.

Sea lion: Like the preceding, but with the head and mane of a lion.

Sea mew: A kind of seagull.

Seapie: A dark-brown water fowl, with red head and white neck and wings.

Seax: A scimitar with a semi-circular notch hollowed out of the back of the blade. A weapon associated with the Saxons who invaded Britain, and whose name is preserved in Essex, Sussex, Middlesex etc. The coats of arms of Essex and Middlesex have seaxes.

Seeded: When roses, lilies etc. are of different tincture.

Segreant: Said of a griffin rampant, wings addorsed.

Sejant or **Segeant:** Sitting.

Sejant addorsed: When two animals are sitting back to back.

Semée: Strewed or powdered with small charges.

Sengreen: A house leek.

Seraph's head: That of a child between three pairs of wings, one pair in chief, one in fesse and one in base.

Serrated: With indentations like those of a saw.

Sexfoil: Like a cinquefoil but with six leaves.

Shackle: A link of a fetter.

Shackbolt: A fetter.

Shafted: Handle of a spear.

Shakefork: Much the same as a pall, but does not touch the edges of the shield.

Sambrough: A kind of slipper.

Shapewined: In a curved line.

Sheaf: *See* **Garb.**

Sheldrake: A variety of duck.

Shivered: Broken or splintered irregularly.

Single: The tail of a deer.

Sinister: Left-hand side (contrast **Dexter**).

Sinople: The French term for vert (green).

Siren or **Syren:** A mermaid.

Shean or **Shene:** A dagger.

Slashed: When the sleeves of a garment are cut open lengthwise, and the apertures show a different colour.

Slay or **Slea:** An instrument used by weavers.

Slipped: Said of leaves and flowers when a slip or stalk is torn from the stem.

Spancelled: When a horse has its fore and hind legs fettered together.

Speed, at: When a stag is shown running.

Sperver: A tent.

Sphinx: A mythical creature with head and breasts of a woman, body of a lion and wings of an eagle.

Spindle: *See* **Fusil.**

Spit: A spade.

Splendour: Said of the sun shown with a human face and irradiated (qv).

Staple: An iron fastening.

Star: *See* **Estoile.**

Starved: Stripped of leaves.

Statant: Standing.

Stellion: A lizard or snake.

Stringed: When an instrument, eg, a bugle horn, has strings of a different tincture.

Sub-ordinaries: *see* **Ordinaries-sub.**

Subverted: Reversed, or turned upside down.

Sufflue: Rest or clarion.

Sun: Shown with a human face, irradiated, and is then called a sun in splendour.

Supporters: Figures placed on either side of a shield.

Surcoat: The coat worn over the armour.

Surgeant: Rising.

Surmounted: When one charge is placed upon another.

Surtout (lit. over all): Said of an escutcheon of pretence.

Swepe: A balista, or machine used for throwing stones.

Swivel: Two iron links which turn on a bolt.

Sykes: A fountain (qv).

Tabard: A surcoat, sleeveless, embroidered with arms and now worn by the heralds in England and Scotland.

Tabernacle: A tent.

Tailed: Said of comets and animals.

Talbot: An old English hunting dog.

Targant, or **Torgant:** Bending or twisting like an S. (*See also* **Torqued.**)

Target: A round shield.

Tasces: The armour which covered the thighs.

Tau: A cross in the shape of the Greek letter 'T'.

Tawny, or **Tenné:** Orange.

Teazel: The head of a kind of thistle.

Tenné: Tawny (*see* above).

Terrace or **Terras:** A narrow mount at the bottom of the base.

Thoye: A lynx.

Threstle or **Trestle:** A three-legged stool.

Thunderbolt: A twisted bar in pale, inflamed at each end, winged and with four forked and barbed darts in saltire issuing from the centre.

Tiara: The Papal mitre.

Tiercé: When the field is divided into three equal areas of different colours.

Timbre: The helmet with wreath, lambrequin and crest, placed over the arms.

Tincture: A heraldic colour; metal or fur.

Tirret or **Turret:** Manacles.

Toison d'or: The Golden Fleece, the badge of the Order of that name.

Torn: A spinning wheel.

Torqued: Wreathed or twisted. (*See* **Targant**).

Torse: The wreath on which the crest is placed.

Torteau: A red roundle.

Torteaux: Discs of colour on a field.

Tortille: Semeé of torteaux.

Tourne: *See* **Reguardant.**

Tower: Triple-towered.

Towered: Having turrets.

Transfixed: Pierced through.

Transfluent: When a stream passes through the arches of a bridge.

Transmuted: Countercharged.

Transpierced: Pierced through.

Transposed: Turned from the ordinary position.

Traversed: Turned to the sinister side.

Trefoiled: As of a cross when its arms end in trefoils, or another ordinary that is edged with trefoils.

Trefoil: A three-leaved grass.

Treillé: Latticed.

Tressure: A diminutive of the orle (half the size).

Tressure flory: A tressure having fleurs-de-lis at intervals around it.

Tressure flory counter flory: The royal tressure in the arms of Scotland, in which alternate fleurs-de-lis point to the centre of the field.

Trevet: A tripod of iron.

Triyle: Formed of three arches.

Tricorporate: When three animals are united in one head in the centre of the shield.

Trident: A long handled fish spear with three prongs.

Trien: Three.

Triparted: Divided into three.

Trippant: When animals of the chase are walking; counter tripping, when two beasts are passing in opposite directions.

Triton: A merman.

Triumphal crown: A crown of laurel leaves.

Trononée: Dismembered (qv).

Truncated: When trees are cut smoothly off at top and bottom.

Trunked: When the trunk is of a different colour.

Trundles: Quills of gold thread.

Trunk of a tree: When the root of the tree has been torn up and the top cut off.

Trussed: Close (qv).

Trussing: When a bird of prey has seized another animal.

Tuberated: Swollen out.

Tun: A barrel.

Turned up: When the lining of a cap is of a different colour and is turned up over one edge.

Turreted: Having small towers.

Tusked: When an animal's tusks are of a different tincture.

Tynes: The branches of the antlers of stags and bucks.

Umbraced or **Umbrated:** Shadowed.

Undée, Undy: Wavy.

Unguled: When the hooves of an animal are of a different tincture.

Unicorn: A mythical animal with the body of a horse, one long twisted horn rising out of its forehead, and with cloven feet.

Unifoil: A single-leaved grass.

Upright: As rampant but applied to reptiles and fish.

Urchin: A hedgehog.

Urinant: Of a fish with head in base.

Urvant or **Urved:** Turned or bowed upwards.

Vair: One of the heraldic furs.

Vallary Crown: Composed of a circle of gold, surmounted by a number of flat pointed strips.

Vambrace: Armour of the arm.

Vambraced: When the arm is covered with armour.

Vamplate, or **Vamplet:** A steel plate fixed on the tilting lance to protect the hand.

Varvelled: When the hawk's jesses have rings at the end.

Verblée: When a hunting horn is edged with metal of a different colour.

Vert: Green.

Verted: Flexed.

Vervels: Small rings.

Vested: Clothed.

View: The track, or footing, of all fallow deer and of a buck.

Vigilance: The stone held by a stork or crane in its uplifted foot.

Vigilant: When a cat is on the lookout for prey.

Visor: The moveable part of a helmet.

Voided: When an ordinary has the interior removed to leave the field visible.

Vol: A pair of wings conjoined.

Volant: Flying.

Vorant (or **Engoulant**): Devouring.

Vulnant: Wounding.

Vulned: Wounded.

Wallet: *See* **Pilgrim's scrip.**

Wastel cakes: Round cakes of bread.

Water bougets (or **budgets**): Vessels to carry water.

Wattled: A term applied to the gills of a cock etc, when the colour has to be mentioned.

Wavy: Formed like waves.

Weare, Weir: Made of stakes and osier twigs interwoven to keep back water.

Wedge: A tool with which to split timber.

Weel: A pot in which to catch fish.

Wellbucket: One with three legs.

Welt (or **Edge**): A narrow border to a charge.

Wervels: Vervels (qv).

Wharrow spindle: Fusil (qv).

Wheatsheaf: *See* **Garb.**

Whirlpool: *See* **Gorges.**

Wings: Having wings.

Wings conjoined: Wings expanded, elevated and united at the base.

Winnowing basket: For winnowing grain.

Wood: Hurst.

Woodman: A savage.

Wreath: That on which the crest is borne, also a garland or chaplet for the head.

Wreathed: Having or wearing a wreath.

Wyvern: A mythical animal with the wings and upper part of a dragon, the lower part with nowed tail as of a snake.

Yale: A mythical creature, coloured argent with spots in gold (or). It is maned, tufted, hoofed, horned and tusked or. The yale is shown by artists as able to swivel its horns at will, so that one horn points forwards and the other backward.

Books to be recommended for future reading:

L. G. Pine
TRACE YOUR ANCESTORS
Evans Bros. Ltd.   Price 5/- (paperback)

THE STORY OF HERALDRY
Charles Tuttle Co. Inc.

INTERNATIONAL HERALDRY
David & Charles Ltd.

INDEX

AINU TRIBES, 44

AKNEY, arms of, 76

ALDERSHOT, borough of, 129

AMBASSADORIAL FUNCTIONS OF HERALDS, 100

ANSTIS, John, 81

ARDEN FAMILY, 99

ARGENTINE, de, 103

Armorial de Berry, 60

ASHBURNHAM FAMILY, 91

ASTRAL CROWN, 13

ATOMIC ENERGY AUTHORITY, arms of the, 133

ATTLEE, Earl, 127

BADGE, ROYAL, for Wales, 106 *et seq*

BALLARD, William, March King of Arms, 105

BARNARD, Dr FP, 55 *et seq*

BARRON, Oswald, 100, 117, 123, 159

BARTHOLUS, (Bartolo of Sassoferato), 21

BAYEUX TAPESTRY, 15 *et seq*, 23

BEAVERBROOK, 47

BERNERS, Dame Juliana, 21, 57

BERRY, William, 64

BLACK PRINCE, arms at Canterbury, 13, 92, 134

BLACKSTONE, William, 81

BLOUNT, John, 55

BODIAM CASTLE, arms on, 87

BOHUN, 80

BOXGROVE, 89

BUCKINGHAM, Edward Stafford, Duke of, 82

BUCKWORTH FAMILY, 39

BUNYAN, John, 101

BURKE, Sir Bernard, 111, 117

BURKE, John, 117

BYSSHE, Sir Edward, 55 *et seq*

CADET, 76

CADENCY, 109

CAERLAVEROCK, Roll of, 49, 109

CALVERLEY, Lord, arms of, 47, 128 *fn*

CANTERBURY, Prerogative Court, 153 *et seq*

CANTING ARMS, 42 *et seq*

CARMINOW, 50 *et seq*

CARTER, Ernest, 133

CENSUS RECORDS, 153 *et seq*

CHANNEL ISLANDS, Heraldry in, 114

CHARLES I, 100

CHARLES II, 81, 100, 110

CHARLES VI (of France), 64

CHESHIRE GC, 58

Cheshire, The Arms of, 134

CHETWYND-STAPYLTON, 36

CHINA, Heraldic, 96

CLAN SYSTEM, 148

CLOTH OF GOLD, Field of, 100

CLOUSTON, J Storer, 48

COACH DOORS, arms on, 95

COKE, Sir Edward, 98

COLE, Col Howard, 129

COLLEGE OF ARMS
    Created, 64, 70
    Records, 156

COMNENA, Anna, 23

CONFIRMATION OF ARMS, 72
    In Ireland, 111

COTHI, Lewis Glyn, 105

COURT OF CHIVALRY, 51, 99

CRESTS, 31

CROMWELL, Oliver, 109

CROMWELL, Thomas, 152

CYMMRODORION SOCIETY, 130

CZECHOSLOVAKIA, 140

D'ABERNON ARMS, 90 *et seq*

DALYNGRIGGE, 13, 88

DAVENPORT FAMILY, 41

DAWES, Elizabeth AS, 23

DIFFERENCE MARKS, 76

DISCLAIMERS OF ARMS, 73

DOMESDAY BOOK, 150 *et seq*

DUGDALE, Sir William, 36, 75 *et seq*

DWNN, Lewis, 106

EARL MARSHAL, 67, 79 *et seq*
EDWARD THE CONFESSOR, 15
EDWARD I, 33, 49 *et seq*
EDWARD III, 56, 68 *et seq*, 135
EDWARD IV, 68
EDWARD VI, 111
ELIZABETH I, 28
ELIZABETH II, 81, 150, 158 *et seq*
ERROLL, Countess of, 59
ESQUIRE AS TITLE, 73, 159
ESSEX ARMS, 139
ETHIOPIA, 146
EUSTACE OF BOULOGNE, 18

FITZWILLIAM, 147
FOUNTAINE, 36
FOX-DAVIES, AC, 22, 39, 93, 98, 110, 111, 118

GALSWORTHY, 24
GARTER KING OF ARMS, 67, 145
GAS COUNCIL, arms of, 132
GAVELKIND, 147 *et seq*
General Armory, 12, 28, 34, 111, 117, 124
GEOFFREY PLANTAGENET, 16
GEORGE III, 135
GEORGE V, 135
GEORGE VI, 13
GILLES LE BOUVIER, 60
GODDARD, Lord, 83 *et seq*
GORGES FAMILY, 42
"GOSS" WARE, 96
GOUGH, Viscount, 45
GRAHAM WINDOW, 110
GRAHAME OF MORPHIE, 38
GROSVENOR, 50 *et seq*
GROSVENOR AND SCROPE, case of, 83
GUILDFORD, John of, 21, 48, 55, 58
GUSTAVUS, Adolphus, 100

HANKEY, 143
HANOVER, 135 *et seq*
HARLEIAN SOCIETY, 71
HARMSWORTH FAMILY, 47, 152
HATCHMENTS, 92
HEADS IN HERALDRY, 43

HEDIN, Sven, 139
HENRY, Prince, 100
HENRY I, 16, 151
HENRY II, 151 *et seq*
HENRY V,
    Writ issued by, 63
    Instituted Garter office, 67, 70
HENRY VII, 64
HENRY VIII, 68, 152
    Commission to Heralds, 71
    And Wales, 148
HERALDRY, Treatises on, 21 *et seq*
HERALDS EXTRAORDINARY, 118, 159
HEREWARD THE WAKE, 144
HERSCHEL, arms of, 47
HEYERDAHL, Thor, 146
HIGH CONSTABLE, Lord, 79 *et seq*
HOOPERS, Messrs, 95
HUME, David, 101, 116

INDIA, Heraldry in, 113
INN SIGNS, 96
INNES OF LEARNEY, Sir Thomas, 115
IRELAND KING OF ARMS, 111
IRISH GENEALOGY, 148
IRISH HERALDRY, 111 *et seq*

JAMES I, 81, 135
JAMES II, 71, 77, 99
JAPAN, Heraldry in, 20
JOHN, King, 18
JOICEY ARMS, 47
JONES, EJ, 58
JONES, Major Francis, 106, 115

KINGSLEY, Charles, 144
KNIGHTS, arms of, 128

LABOUR PEERS, arms of, 127
LIVERIES, 93
LONDON, H Stanford, 60
LORD LYON, 85, 108, 110, 115
LUCY ARMS, 46 *et seq*
LUTTRELL ARMS, 14
LYNCH-ROBINSON, Sir Christopher, 22, 115
LYON OFFICE, 110, 145

McKIE FAMILY, 42
MACLAGAN, Sir Eric, 23
MADOX FAMILY, 105
MALET ARMS, 138
MALTA, 114
Manchester City v. Manchester Palace of Varieties, 83 *et seq*
MAORIS, 146
MARTIN, 38
MATRICULATION (in Scotland), 109 *et seq*
MIKADOS, 146
MONCREIFFE, Sir Iain, 11, 22, 115
MONTGOMERY, Viscount, 104
MORIARTY, G Andrews, 122
MOTTOES, 37

NAMES AND ARMS CLAUSES, 82
NATIONAL COAL BOARD, arms of, 131
NATIONALISED INDUSTRIES, arms of, 131 *et seq*
NELSON, Lord, arms of, 102
NEW ENGLAND HISTORIC GENEALOGICAL SOCIETY, 122
NIALL OF THE NINE HOSTAGES, 148
NICOLAS, Sir Harris, 54
NORFOLK, Duke of, 67

OFFICERS OF ARMS, origin of, 67 *et seq*
ORDINARIES, 38

PARISH REGISTERS, 152
PETRA SANCTA SYSTEM, 118
PILKINGTON FAMILY, 41
POLISH HERALDRY, 140
PRESCRIPTIVE RIGHT TO ARMS, 74 *et seq*
PROBATE COURT, 153
PUBLIC RECORD OFFICE, 154
PURPLE HEART, 125

RESPITE FOR PROOF, 74
RICHARD I, 19, 48, 135
RICHARD II, 53, 111
RICHARD III, 63 *et seq*
RIDDARHUSET, 140
ROLLS OF ARMS,
    In England, 48
    In America, 122

ROMAN ANCESTRY, 19, 145
ROMANTIC REVIVAL, 116
ROYAL AIR FORCE BADGES, 13

ST DAVID'S, Viscount, 160
ST ETHELDREDA'S CHURCH, 96
ST GEORGE, family of, 100, 161
ST JOHN OF BLETSO, 161
ST JUST, arms, 161
ST PAUL, 147
SCOTT, Sir Walter, 116, 144
SCOTT-GILES, CW, 22, 99
SCOTS HERALDRY, 107 *et seq*
Scrope v Grosvenor, 50 *et seq*
SEALS, 16 *et seq*
SEGOVIA ARMS, 138
SHAKESPEARE, William, 28, 98 *et seq*
SIGNET RINGS, 94
SOMERSET HOUSE, 153 *et seq*
SPEKE, William, 36
SPELMANN, Sir Henry, 55
STANDISH, Robert, 20
STENTON, Sir Frank, 147
STOURTON, 40
SUPPORTERS, 35 *et seq*
SURROGATE FOR EARL MARSHAL, 83 *et seq*
SWEDISH ARMS, 139

TAX ON ARMS, 82, 159
TORRANCE FAMILY, 44
TOTEMS, 44
TOURNAMENTS, 100
TRAFFORD, 41, 144

ULSTER KING OF ARMS, 111 *et seq*
UPTON, Nicholas, 21, 55
URWICK ORR AND PARTNERS LTD, 130
USER, as giving right to arms, 75

VESPASIAN, 145
VICTORIA, Queen, 135, 158
VISITATIONS, Heralds', 33, 67 *et seq*, 99,
    In Wales, 105
    In Ireland, 111 *et seq*
    And pedigrees, 143